PRAISE FOR *INTENTIONAL MINDSET*

"Having played in the NBA for many years, I know a killer instinct when I see one. You can almost sense it. Dave not only has a killer instinct himself but he's great at teaching you the principles to find yours, too. I highly recommend this book to anyone looking to better themselves and develop a true killer instinct and mental toughness."

—Meyers Leonard, NBA's Miami Heat

"At first glance, it's easy to find Dave's characters, Frances, Frank or Fred, in those we work with. But in typical Dave fashion, as he carries us along, we begin to find morsels of ourselves in each of them. That's when we begin to learn."

—Troy Tomlinson, CEO of Universal Music Publishing Group, Nashville

"I've seen firsthand the results that come from being absolutely captivated by the mentality of mental toughness and destroying the excuses of adversity that Dave Anderson teaches and lives. Dave puts you front and center inside these pages to gain the tools and attitude you need to lead a life and profession that embraces challenges and knocks out fear and doubts."

—Tom Crean, head coach of the Georgia Bulldogs

"*Intentional Mindset* is a truly excellent road map for people to follow, who want to raise their awareness of identifying the gaps that they may have, in their approach to realizing greater levels of success in their lives. Success in anything requires a plan. The knowledge shared by Dave Anderson in this book shows you how to put this plan together to make it a part of your activities each day. It offers a healthy way to self-evaluate one's actions in success and failure to work toward continuous improvement in all the things that we deem important in our lives. It also shows how to develop better mental toughness and killer instinct by focusing one's attitude as to how to engage with events that work against them."

—Brad Bartlett, president of Dole Packaged Foods

"Dave's grasp on developing lifelong leadership qualities is outstanding. He brings a real-world honest approach to combating instant gratification leadership in all facets of life. This book will not only equip the leaders of tomorrow but will also help those in leadership positions today strengthen and solidify their mental toughness and killer instinct."

—Jason Loscalzo, head strength and conditioning coach for the Chicago Bears

"We all have the ability to have a killer instinct; it's inside each and every one of us and this book helps us identify it, empower it and develop it. In the current world, those that do so will have the competitive advantage needed to stay ahead. I personally started reading Dave Anderson's books more than a decade ago, and they helped me understand that my business is my responsibility, not to make excuses, and winners WIN. Family First Life in seven short years has gone from issuing $7 million to $400 million in policies this year, and the lessons I have learned from Mr. Anderson's books and the training he provides to our entire company annually are a big reason why. The world is changing. Don't get left behind. Develop the killer instinct that is inside you and this book has a road map showing you exactly how to do so. Thank you, Dave, this is another must-read for those looking to WIN."

—Shawn Meaike, president of Family First Life Insurance Company

INTENTIONAL MINDSET

ALSO BY DAVE ANDERSON

Unstoppable: Transforming Your Mindset to Create Change, Accelerate Results, and Be the Best at What You Do

It's Not Rocket Science: 4 Simple Strategies for Mastering the Art of Execution

How to Lead by THE BOOK: Proverbs, Parables, and Principles to Tackle Your Toughest Business Challenges

How to Run Your Business by THE BOOK (Revised and Expanded): A Biblical Blueprint to Bless Your Business

How to Run Your Business by THE BOOK: A Biblical Blueprint to Bless Your Business

TKO Hiring! Ten Knockout Strategies for Recruiting, Interviewing, and Hiring Great People

TKO Sales! Ten Knockout Strategies for Selling More of Anything

TKO Management! Ten Knockout Strategies for Becoming the Manager Your People Deserve

Up Your Business! 7 Steps to Fix, Build, or Stretch Your Organization (Second Edition, Revised and Expanded)

How to Deal with Difficult Customers: 10 Simple Strategies for Selling to the Stubborn, Obnoxious, and Belligerent

If You Don't Make Waves You'll Drown: 10 Hard-Charging Strategies for Leading in Politically Correct Times

Up Your Business! 7 Steps to Fix, Build, or Stretch Your Organization

No-Nonsense Leadership: Real World Strategies to Maximize Personal & Corporate Potential

Selling Above the Crowd: 365 Strategies for Sales Excellence

INTENTIONAL MINDSET

Developing Mental Toughness and a Killer Instinct

DAVE ANDERSON

Matt Holt Books
An Imprint of BenBella Books, Inc.
Dallas, TX

Matt Holt Books is an imprint of BenBella Books, Inc.
BenBella Books, Inc.
10440 N. Central Expressway
Suite 800
Dallas, TX 75231
benbellabooks.com
Send feedback to feedback@benbellabooks.com

Printed in the United States of America
10 9 8 7 6 5 4 3 2 1

Library of Congress Control Number: 2020046003
ISBN 9781953295026 (trade cloth)
ISBN 9781953295217 (electronic)

Copyediting by Elizabeth Degenhard
Proofreading by Lisa Story and Marissa Uhrina
Text design and composition by Aaron Edmiston
Cover design by Heather Butterfield
Cover photo © Shutterstock / Mega Pixel
Printed by Lake Book Manufacturing
Distributed to the trade by Two Rivers Distribution, an Ingram brand
tworiversdistribution.com

Intentional Mindset *is dedicated to the following special people:*

To my friend and Red Belt Brother, Damian Lillard, a mental toughness legend and killer instinct icon.

To Coach Howard Moore, whose resilience and example motivated a level of killer instinct and mental toughness within a group of young men that helped shape them as champions.

To my UNFAZED Red Belt Badger Brothers:

Brad (Blaze), Micah (Big Jam), D'Mitrik (Meech), Nate (Nuke), Aleem (Beast), Brevin (Dagger), Trevor (Pitbull), Walt (Punch), Tyler (Scrap), Mike (Bull), Joe (Vike), Carter, Owen, Courtland, Samad, Greg (Silent Assassin), Deani, Joe, Alando, Erik, Henry, Marc, Kyle, Kevin, AJ.

Ethan, Khalil, and Chuck.

CONTENTS

FOREWORD

It took me nearly a whole year to connect with Dave Anderson once I learned who he was and obtained his contact information. I hesitated to call him because I knew it would lead to a potential appearance in front of my team, and I have always been cautiously skeptical of who I allow speak to my guys. Dave came highly recommended by Tom Crean, who was the head basketball coach at Indiana University at the time. His assistant coaches raved about Dave too, which was even better to hear as I knew I'd get the cold, hard truth from other staff members. As I polled others across college basketball who knew of Dave, I kept getting the same message—"get him in front of your team." Finally, in August 2017 I picked up the phone and dialed the number I'd held for several months.

Interestingly, as we talked on the phone, I found myself agreeing with all he was talking about regarding motivation, growth, overcoming adversity, and so on. I had just gotten a copy of his book *Unstoppable* and hadn't read it thoroughly yet, but I had to pretend like I had. Following about a ten-minute conversation, I hung up the phone and was determined to do a deeper dive to learn more about his viewpoints and tactics but knew his messaging would resonate with my team if they were really listening and "bought in."

Fast forward more than eighteen months later, to Friday, January 18, 2019. Dave Anderson and I finally connected hours before he would make his first appearance in front of my team. We were not playing up to our potential, having lost four out of our last five. We had a "whininess" about us—too many guys feeling "woe is me," too many pity parties. We were stuck in neutral and just weren't mentally mature nor tough enough to get over the hump. Oh, and we had undefeated (17–0) and number two–ranked Michigan staring us in the face in Madison the very next day.

Following that day's practice, post-practice meal, and recovery time, Dave took center stage in our video room in front of our players and staff. For the next two hours, he was fantastic. He told his life story to connect all the dots for the observers and gave a quick history lesson on how he got to where he is. Needless to say, Dave had the full and undivided attention of every single person in that room. The story of his past, his life's adversity, and all that he's overcome was a remarkably inspirational listen. His stories and the power of "WHY" helped chase away some of the insecurities and immaturities with which our team was struggling. His challenge of developing a "Red Belt Mindset" was exactly what the doctor ordered for this team and where we were mentally at that given point of the year. We needed a good mental "kick in the ass" and coinciding wake-up call. Dave delivered one right between the eyes. I didn't intentionally wait until we were struggling to bring Dave in, but we couldn't have scripted his appearance and messaging to my team any better if we tried.

Now, I won't give *all* the credit to Dave for the next day's 64–54 beating of Michigan, because we had good players step up and play well, made big plays down the stretch, and put away the nation's last undefeated team that afternoon. But there was no doubt we had a depth of fire and mental toughness to us that had previously failed to show itself consistently. My ego would say "good coaching," but I knew deep down that we had struck a chord on the mental keyboard of our team, all in a good, positive, challenging way. We would go on to win the next five in a row. Always drawing back on Dave's message of "What's your Why?" and the "Red Belt Mindset," we clawed our way back into Big Ten contention and returned to the NCAA tournament later that spring.

Since that cold January night in 2019, Dave has connected with our team on a variety of occasions, always imparting a message that's inspiring and motivating, leaving anyone who is feeling sorry for themselves ducking for cover or in a mad rush to change their ways.

When Dave asked me to write the foreword for *Intentional Mindset*, I was unbelievably honored. I know you'll hear a few nuggets of our struggles with many adversities throughout the 2019–2020 season and beyond. There's no doubt that Dave's influence and echoing messages helped pull us through tough times. Although maybe we didn't completely stop sulking, pouting, or having a "woe is me" moment from time to time (it's human nature), we were doing it far less and often autocorrected ourselves if we started to wobble off the tracks. Those seeds of toughness and resiliency planted over a year before helped pave the way to our 2020 Big Ten Conference basketball championship.

I know you'll enjoy *Intentional Mindset* and hope it can help springboard your life, team, organization, or family in ways similar to how Dave Anderson has helped my Wisconsin Badgers!

Greg Gard
Head Coach of the
University of Wisconsin
Men's Basketball team

INTRODUCTION

Congratulations are in order: Buying this book demonstrates you already have the killer instinct to want to improve yourself and your life. Finishing the book will make evident that you have the mental toughness to endure life's many demands and distractions and still complete what's important to you.

When we are not where we believe we should be in our lives, we can feel a sense of inspirational dissatisfaction nudging us toward something better, and more. This dynamic can create a mental tension where although we are grateful for what we have and have accomplished, we also sense that we can become better: in our career; in our health; as a spouse, parent, or friend; or in our own growth trajectory. In spite of this, we can too often display the same thinking and tendencies that year after year have held us back. If you are in this state from time to time, or feel stuck there now, you can move forward after you intentionally change how you think.

MOVE FROM INCIDENTAL TO INTENTIONAL

Intentional is a word you will see often throughout this book. Defined as "done on purpose; deliberate,"[1] it may help to think of intentionality in this context: If you want to get into shape physically, you would consistently follow an intentional process, over time, that causes you to start doing things you haven't done, and to stop doing things that inhibit reaching your goal. Obviously, building a dream body would not be as simple or fast as eating a single salad, refusing one dessert, doing five push-ups, getting a great night's sleep, and then declaring yourself "fit for life." Nor could you expect to awaken after one day of physical discipline to discover you had developed six-pack abs or could win a marathon.

Our mindset, "the established set of attitudes held by someone," works in a similar way.[2] While we understand the diligent, intentional, "slow cooker" method for reaching physical goals, many act like they can "microwave" a healthier mindset and instantly change their life by taking good notes at a seminar, reading a "quote of the day," or hanging motivational posters on their walls. Just as improving a physique requires intentionality, consistency, time, evaluation, adjustments, and trade-offs, so too does changing and building a mindset that makes you continually superior in performance to your former self in life's most essential arenas. And that is the essence and purpose behind this book—to help you become more intentional and less incidental when it comes to developing the killer instinct and mental toughness necessary to achieve your most essential goals.

DEVELOP YOUR ONE-TWO PUNCH

Killer instinct: "An aggressive, tenacious urge to dominate in a struggle to attain a goal."[3]

Mental toughness: A measure of confidence and resilience predictive of success in education, athletics, or the workplace.

Think of killer instinct and mental toughness as the "one-two punch" that accelerates success and knocks out complacency, with killer instinct being the impetus that "gets you started" and mental toughness being the driving force that powers you to fight to the finish.

Keeping in mind the insight I previously shared on the concepts of intentionality and mindset, if we were to structure these together with killer instinct and mental toughness into a first-person affirmative paragraph that could become your personal mantra—one that changes how you think and gets you past the same old habits and tendencies that have held you back—it might look something like this:

> I will intentionally establish an unfazed mindset and attack my most significant life goals, persisting through obstacles until I achieve them. My foremost objective is to compete every day with my former self—to become more as a person—so that I can achieve more in all life's essential arenas: relationships, health, finances, family, spirituality, the workplace. As I purposefully upgrade critical success traits, I'll build a confidence and resilience that makes me unstoppable as I fight to achieve what matters most to me and those I love.

IT WORKS IF YOU WORK IT

At *Intentional Mindset's* conclusion you will find an optional, but highly recommended, ten-week, ACCREDITED course as post-book follow-through, which will guide you to work on ten key success traits essential to building an intentional mindset that increases your killer instinct and mental toughness. During the course you will devote one week's work to each of the ten traits, and the attributes you will work to improve form the acronym ACCREDITED: attitude, competitiveness, character, rigor, effort, discipline, intelligence, tenacity, energy, and drive.

Tempting as it may be to immediately dive into the course, I recommend you completely read *Intentional Mindset* before you begin the seventy-day course so that you are better able to understand how the ACCREDITED traits intersect with and support one another.

THE POWER OF PROCESS

The ACCREDITED course and process was inspired by eighteenth-century America's Benjamin Franklin. As you may be aware, Franklin was an American statesman, businessman, philosopher, author, inventor, and founding father . . . all despite only two years of formal education.[4] One of seventeen children, Franklin dropped out of school at the age of ten to work in his father's candle making business.[5] After such limited schooling, he committed early in life to intentional self-improvement and around 1728, in his early twenties, developed a list of thirteen virtues he would work to develop, at a pace of one per week, including daily evaluation and adjusting.[6] He then would repeat the process four times throughout the year.[7] While some ACCREDITED traits are the same or similar to Franklin's, others have been consolidated or edited to fit this book's specific purpose of improving killer instinct and building mental toughness.

As Franklin followed his intentional self-improvement process, he went on to become America's first self-made millionaire, making his fortune in the publishing business. His most famous works, *Poor Richard's Almanac* and *The Autobiography of Benjamin Franklin*, continue to sell well to this day. In addition to signing the Declaration of Independence, Franklin was the first United States postmaster general, the first US ambassador to both Sweden and France, and governor of Pennsylvania. His inventions included bifocals, the lightning rod, the Franklin Stove, the glass harmonica, and a flexible urinary tract catheter. He was arguably America's first renaissance man, an eighteenth-century rock star! His timeless and intentional process is proven and principle-driven, transcending generations, continents, and cultures.

THE BIG PICTURE

The first three chapters cover developing the two qualities I introduced earlier: killer instinct and mental toughness. They likewise lay the groundwork for *Intentional Mindset* because the need for greater killer instinct, mental toughness, and the motivations that fuel them to new levels is near universal for anyone trying to accomplish a worthwhile goal: studying for an A; seeking the right mate or breaking off a toxic relationship; losing weight; earning a martial arts rank promotion; learning another language; executing do-it-yourself projects; rearing a child; raising a teenager; trying to make an athletic team, earn a scholarship, or become MVP; launching a new business; vying for a sales account; aspiring for a promotion; switching careers; trying to change the world through activism; starting a church; desiring to stay focused, positive, and productive during a crisis like the COVID-19 pandemic; and so on.

Chapter four, "Decisions Determine Direction," highlights the impact of one's personal decisions over external conditions on higher levels of killer instinct and mental toughness. A dependence on conditions can make you feel victimized when they are unfavorable, and this chapter will focus you on making more consistently productive daily decisions. As General George Patton famously said, "When a decision has to be made, make it. There is no totally right time for anything."[8] To that I would add that right decisions can create better conditions, and those decisions are within your direct control, while the conditions may not be.

Ten subsequent chapters are devoted to the ten individual ACCREDITED traits, with each teaching and presenting further insights into developing that particular trait. For example, the seven aspects of improving your attitude that we will cover are:

- Responding productively to negative things or people
- The art of not being easily offended
- Developing the discipline to demonstrate positive speech
- Developing a laser focus on what you can control
- Learning to maintain grace under stress
- Refusing to engage in blame and excuses
- Boosting others and lifting yourself

Overview of the ACCREDITED Chapters

Chapter Five: **Attitude:** Build a Stronger ABLE So You're Able to Go Stronger
Chapter Six: **Competitiveness:** Go from Common Participant to Commonly Dominant
Chapter Seven: **Character:** Cultivate a Rock-Solid Moral Code
Chapter Eight: **Rigor:** Design a Relentless Daily Regimen
Chapter Nine: **Effort:** Work Harder Smarter and Smarter Harder
Chapter Ten: **Discipline:** Become a No-Nonsense Master of "No'ing"
Chapter Eleven: **Intelligence:** Grow Your Smarts Before Stupidity Starts
Chapter Twelve: **Tenacity:** Hone a Rock-Hardheadedness
Chapter Thirteen: **Energy:** Fuel a Fanatical Focus and Fight to the Finish
Chapter Fourteen: **Drive:** Become a Driven Driver, Not a Driver Who's Driven

While perusing the ACCREDITED traits you will work to develop, you may have rightly surmised this is not simply another "business" book, but a *life* book, one that will help you grow in all key arenas of your life: family, friendships, finances, workplace, athletics, spirituality, health, and more.

The final chapters of *Intentional Mindset* begin with a case study recounting the application of this book's principles, based on the real-life journey of the 2019–2020 University of Wisconsin Badgers men's basketball team—through a season of incomparable and unrelenting adversity—and serves as a call to action to leverage your momentum after completing the book and follow through with the ACCREDITED process. I began my association with the team a year prior in a mental skills capacity, working with the players to develop more killer instinct and mental toughness. At the conclusion of *Intentional Mindset*, you will be presented with an overview of how your ten-week growth journey will progress and steps on how to customize the follow-up course to fit your needs and opportunities.

Sprinkled throughout the chapters is an assortment of ***BIG*** **(Be Intentionally Great) Bullets**. These highlighted outtakes make, expand on, or reinforce specific points related to the material at hand. Here are a couple of examples:

BIG Bullet: It doesn't matter if you don't "feel" like it. Your goals don't care if you are tired.

BIG Bullet: Adversity births seeds of benefit most people never water.

Each chapter concludes with an **Intentional Action** assignment that will help you get more from what you just read and apply it purposefully. If you execute these assignments, you not only will gain deeper understanding and knowledge of the subject matter, but will build the discipline to prepare you for, and help you get the most from, the ACCREDITED course.

"PLAY A POOR HAND WELL"

Likewise, as a separate outtake at the conclusions of chapters one through fourteen, I will present one challenge (fourteen in total) that the Wisconsin Badgers men's basketball team endured and had to overcome individually and as a team during the 2019–2020 season. Your task will be to evaluate how you can deal with your own version of those particular setbacks, disappointments, losses, or adversities. Each "Badgers Adversity Incident" presented will build to a conclusion in chapter fifteen, where I will relate how the team itself handled these attacks on their killer instinct and mental toughness, the lessons learned, and outcomes.

THE HARD TRUTH

As you prepare to read the book, I want to encourage you that whatever capacities or abilities you have currently in the ACCREDITED categories *are not fixed.* They can be improved, and you will succeed in that endeavor as you intentionally apply what you learn and make necessary adjustments as you read the book and throughout the seventy days of self-work. As human beings, we develop to our potential when there is structure, not when we are winging it, trying to will our way through obstacles to achieve a goal, or shooting from the hip and spontaneously making our life up as we daily stumble along. So, follow the structure, because structure matters! Structure provides the guardrails to lead you down the right path and prevent you from taking a wrong turn throughout the process.

If you have ever attended one of my live presentations, read one of my past books, or listened to our podcast, *The Game Changer Life*, you also know a bit about my communication style: I get right to the point, and I disdain political correctness and the dishonesty that accompanies much of it. You can expect me to be direct with you, honest with you, and unafraid to make you uncomfortable by sharing hard truths. In fact, the aspects of this book that make you the most uncomfortable may have the most to teach you.

But I want you to know that the reason I am writing this book—with a format unlike any of the fourteen I have written previously—is not for more money or fame, or because I just feel it is time for another book. I am writing it because after over two decades of teaching and applying success principles throughout the world I have come to see more clearly that often the glaring differences between those who continually grow and those who stay stuck or regress come from a disparity in commitment to *intentionality* and *consistency* in life's vital disciplines, resulting in vastly different levels of killer instinct and/or mental toughness.

Chapter One

KILLER INSTINCT GETS YOU STARTED

FRED, FRANK, AND FRANCES

Meet Fred, Frank, and Frances: They work together in the same nationally known retail sales organization, and their personalities and characteristics are representative of persons on teams everywhere in business, athletics, nonprofits, and more. They all share the same leader, teammates, workplace, schedule, economy, opportunities, products, and more; and yet, their results differ tremendously. While there are many ostensible reasons for these differences, the primary cause—varying degrees of killer instinct and mental toughness—represents their biggest performance separators. We will revisit this trio later in chapter two in the context of discovering why Frank has a higher level of killer instinct quotient than Fred, and why Frances's killer instinct beats Frank's and has made her the long-running sales champ in her organization. The "retail sales team" context, and the ensuing lessons learned from these three and their performance, are applicable for all businesses and nonprofits and those in education, athletics, and more.

THE CORRECT CORE CAUSE

Deficient killer instinct and mental toughness are the core causes of achievement shortfalls most often attributed to conditions such as the following: "bad breaks," "bad luck," "bad plan," "bad genes," "bad upbringing," "wrong goals," "wrong job," "wrong boss," "wrong timing," "wrong team," "fickle father," "mean momma," and more. An enemy of personal progress and growth I call "unconscious complacency" gives stagnation a foothold in your life and can make the dreams you once envisioned, or currently aspire to, in relationships, finances, fitness, the workplace, and more seem always out of reach or even impossible. There will be more on complacency shortly, but, suffice to say, its threat needs to be on your radar.

Since our biggest vulnerability is the one of which we are unaware, an important first step to jumpstart or accelerate progress and growth begins with overcoming the pull of complacency, and developing and leveraging greater measures of killer instinct and mental toughness. While it's common to blame or credit genetics, parents, upbringing, nature, personality, schooling, ethnicity, gender, age, bad breaks, or rotten luck for our performance successes or disappointments, history is filled with substantial stories of both failure and success from people your same age, gender, personality, ethnicity, with similar schooling, parents, genetics, and lousy breaks and luck. While those factors, depending on whether they are favorable or not, can either help or hinder your journey, the primary responsibility for progress and growth lies within you, and it starts with how you choose to think, the subsequent decisions you make, and the most consistent actions you take. As Ben Franklin put it, ". . . the happiness and good of all men consists in right action, and right action cannot be produced without right opinion."[9]

Killer instinct means having an aggressive, tenacious urge to attain a goal. In contrast, mental toughness is the confidence and resilience that sustains you as you work toward that goal. One doesn't substitute for the other; it partners with it. As I mentioned in the introduction, killer instinct gets you started, putting you into action mode toward a goal, and mental toughness helps get you finished, powering you to persist with the journey until you achieve the goal despite the disappointments, setbacks, losses, or defeats throughout the process. Many people have a high level of either killer instinct or mental toughness, but not strong quotients of both. As a result, they may become successful to a point in both areas but completely fall short of the more significant success that consistent progress and growth would have brought them.

BIG Bullet: Having strong killer instinct means no one has to give you pep talks or incentives to get you going because you're already going. Any external motivation just gets you going faster.

SUPPLEMENTS, NOT SYNONYMS OR SUBSTITUTES

Killer instinct and mental toughness are frequently discussed in places ranging from job interviews to employee evaluations, locker rooms, and seminars, but their unique roles are often confused or misunderstood. People with strong killer instinct but low mental toughness are often starting things with much vigor and enthusiasm but fizzle out over time and move on to something else when the process gets tough or mundane. Those with strong levels of mental toughness and low killer instinct need immense prompting, threats, begging, or bribes to get going, but once they are in motion and striving toward an objective, they latch onto it like a starving dog onto a pork chop, gnawing away until he's finished every marrowed morsel. While we are born with enough killer instinct and mental toughness to cry when we are hungry and persist until we're fed, here is what I hope encourages you: Killer instinct and mental toughness can both be substantially elevated by intent coupled with the process presented in this book. No one can do it for you, but you can do it for yourself.

BIG Bullet: If something can be developed, it is within your control. From there, whether you progress, regress, or plateau is on you. And you shouldn't want it any other way.

THE SILENT ASSASSIN OF PERSONAL POTENTIAL

The archenemy of both killer instinct and mental toughness is complacency. Complacency presents a persistent and pervasive ambush to progress and growth. It is defined as being calmly content; smugly self-satisfied.[10] Many wrongly believe that complacent means "lazy," but that is not how it works. In fact, you can labor tirelessly at the task at hand, yet be so calmly content with your process or progress that you never change, improve, risk, or innovate. Being complacent or not isn't so much about the number of hours or days you put in each week as it is *what* you are putting into those hours and days, whether it's on the practice court, in the workplace, or at home with your family.

In the simplest terms, complacency is about being comfortable with the status quo and as a result being less likely to extend yourself beyond your comfort zone to attack, change, or work harder or smarter. Some folks remain financially broke or professionally underperforming because they have become comfortable in that situation; they have learned to live with it. It used to hurt, but now it feels normal. Others live comfortably being average or slightly better at what they do, so they resist change or risk that would upset that contentment. Likewise, others become successful beyond what they ever imagined for themselves, yet still never achieve what they ultimately could have because they allow prosperity to drain their drive. They get to the top of the mountain and build a vacation home there rather than look to climb a higher mountain.

The comfort zone that complacency creates is nurtured and expands in the absence of crisis or struggles beyond what we have learned to deal with—in other words, when life or business is manageable and the seas appear calm. For as much as human beings crave and pursue prosperity, it has a knack for sapping urgency and causing them to let up on vital disciplines and habits that made them initially prosperous, opening the door for calm contentedness and smug satisfaction to sneak into their lives and stultify progress and growth. The comfort they feel in their situation becomes a seductress that lulls them into a dream-killing, steady-as-she-goes, don't-rock-the-boat mindset. They start playing not to lose, instead of playing to win, to win big, and to win it all.

Complacency doesn't announce itself with a left jab to the jaw, but instead gradually and consistently desensitizes and impairs one's thinking and behaviors over time, one poor decision or abandoned discipline at a time. It truly is the silent assassin of human potential. Complacency's alluring power is why most folks stagnate too often and for too long. It's the threat they never see coming or identify, even when engulfed by it, which is why I refer to it as "unconscious" complacency. Because people do not recognize the problem, they don't face it, and since they don't face it, they cannot fix it. Becoming unconsciously complacent is why good performers never become great and why even the great stop far short of their best. Perhaps the number one thing many accomplished people wrongly believe is that complacency is the problem of someone else—an underachiever or perhaps a sluggard. But that is not how it works. Complacency does not discriminate based on age, gender, ethnicity, social status, education level, income, performance ranking, or career field. *All* are susceptible because all are prone to follow the natural tendency to maintain or seek comfort versus the unnatural action of seeking out the discomfort that precedes growth. After all, discomfort upsets a status quo we are accustomed to—one that is certain and without the anxiety of the unknown.

BIG Bullet: Believing complacency isn't a threat or problem for you is a clear sign you're unconsciously complacent.

Complacency in life's various arenas—health, work, finances, relationships, spirituality—can, and will, infect all of us occasionally. We're human. It happens. But it is important to understand that complacency works much like a staged disease: It is easier to combat with early detection. However, because complacent people are often doing well in at least some areas in their life, the absence of a crisis that would jolt them out of their comfort zone blinds them to their complacency until they either hit a plateau or decline manifests. Given enough time, a comfort zone becomes a casket that buries your dreams, personal potential, and that best life you could have had. While the unconsciously complacent often remain successful in the world's eyes, notwithstanding their affliction, complacency ensures they miss out on the growth and progress they could have attained had they continued to hone their killer instinct and mental toughness. And despite the common deathbed laments over what "could have been" or "should have been" in one's life, the brutal truth is that no other person or external condition restrains the masses from reaching their fullest potential.

Rather, the hapless hordes simply remain unaware or unconcerned and don't realize they need to get out of their own way to be able to break from the comfortable state they are in to achieve the success for which they were designed. As is so common, they lacked the awareness, desire, or process (maybe all three) that would have helped them intentionally create a mindset to get comfortable being uncomfortable and become their best in the process.

LET UP OR STEP UP?

As you candidly reflect on your own life up to this point, what happens to your level of killer instinct when prosperity graces your path in your work, relationships, health, finances, or otherwise? Do you let up or step up? Do you strategically recharge and then re-charge, or do you rest so long that you rust? Have you unintentionally embraced the "I've arrived," "I'm doing better than I used to," or the "I must be doing something right" mental exhale too often used as an excuse to not extend yourself or change—unwittingly flipping your allegiance from rigor and discipline to ease and instant gratification? If so, I can assure you that you can do better and will discover just how much more so in the coming weeks as you complete this book and take action with the ACCREDITED course.

Or perhaps you have lived a life where you cannot remember ever *not* struggling for long, have rarely enjoyed abundance, and are now so accustomed to mediocrity, getting by, or feeling stuck that you have become unconsciously complacent in your misery. If so, you too are designed for more than this and will likewise discover just how much more so in due time.

While you would never wade into either of the aforementioned complacency scenarios with a masochistic intent for self-sabotage, the chances are that over time you gradually started to settle for what is easier, cheaper, popular, convenient, or comfortable, and stopped exploring a more intentional, more productive, harder path to systematically stretch yourself, create a healthy discomfort, and accelerate progress and growth over time.

Regardless of where you are now on your life journey, you have already developed certain levels of killer instinct and mental toughness throughout your life that have helped you work through struggles and accomplish goals. And you can build on that. The fact that you are reading this book demonstrates you are not content with the status quo and are open to extending yourself with what may be uncomfortable. By the time you have finished this and the next chapters you will be fortified with a foundation for following a calculated, seventy-day blueprint that no longer leaves igniting the killer instinct and developing the mental toughness needed to change your life to chance, but guides you to proactively work on yourself more purposefully and intensely.

BIG Bullet: While you can't start your life journey over again, you can start fresh today and create a new end.

SOMETHING HAS GOT TO CHANGE

Settling for where we are in life—financially, vocationally, physically, spiritually, with relationships, and more—happens one letup, one compromise, one preference for the instant gratification of what's safe over what's unknown, at a time. We say we feel stuck, but no one "stuck" us. We dug the ditch one misguided decision or indecision after another and learned to live with the easier *known* than the scary *uncomfortable*. At first, we may have felt like we would get back after a better life someday, but "someday" became "one of these days," and one of these days turned into none of these days. If we are honest with ourselves, we admit that settling for where we were was just a sneakier, more creative way of quitting.

Three Big Ifs

- If what used to hurt, bother us, or nag a little has started to feel normal, that is a wake-up call that something has got to change.
- If we have memories bigger than our dreams, something has got to change.
- If we realize we climbed a mountain, pitched a retirement tent there, and never looked for a new peak to climb, something has got to change.

That something is you. Consider these three points that take the ball of life and put it squarely in your court:

1. Nothing is going to change for you until something changes *within* you, starting with a clearer, more compelling *WHY* that motivates you to create a more intentional mindset, stronger mental toughness, and a killer instinct.
2. Nothing is going to change for you until something changes *about* you, starting with how you choose to spend your gift of time each day and with whom you choose to spend it.
3. It's time to stop waiting for something to change for you and change something within you and about you, so you can change what's around you. When that happens, things are less likely to happen to you and you will start happening to things. You will live life as the proactive boxer, not the complacent punching bag, and start hitting back against unconscious complacency—that relentless, ubiquitous, silent assassin of the life you were designed to live.

INTENTIONAL ACTION

Be intentional, and write down in a journal or Word document the areas of your life where you believe you have become complacent now or have historically had problems being complacent, where you were calmly content or smugly self-satisfied:

- eating habits
- overall health maintenance (dental and physical checkups)
- physical exercise
- stronger relationships with your spouse, kids, family, or friends
- maintenance of your cars, homes, or other assets
- financial disciplines like budgeting or saving
- retirement planning
- work or job disciplines

- spiritual disciplines
- personal growth disciplines, and more

Going forward, you will convert what you have listed in this exercise into improvement objectives in the Intentional Action section of chapter two.

BADGERS ADVERSITY INCIDENTS AND PLAY A POOR HAND WELL

As mentioned in the introduction, the conclusion of each chapter will relate an incident of adversity, disappointment, or a setback the Wisconsin Badgers men's basketball team endured during their 2019–2020 season. Each Play a Poor Hand Well section builds to a conclusion in chapter fifteen, which will relate how the team handled the incidents, the lessons learned, and the season's outcome.

Based on the knowledge you have acquired, your goal after reading each section is to evaluate how you can deal with your own version of these particular adversities and influence others on your team (family, workplace, athletic team, and the like) to do likewise. The incidents are listed in chronological order as the season progressed.

BADGERS ADVERSITY INCIDENT #1

May 25, 2019: Coach Howard Moore Family Automobile Tragedy

During the off-season, at 2:04 AM on May 25, 2019, the vehicle driven by beloved Badgers assistant coach Howard Moore and his family was struck by a drunk driver speeding the wrong way down a Michigan highway. Moore's wife, Jennifer, and nine-year-old daughter, Jaidyn, were killed, and his son, Jerrell, was injured. Coach Moore suffered devastating injuries including second- and third-degree burns to his head and face, and slipped into a coma.

PLAY A POOR HAND WELL

When extreme adversity strikes you or those you love:

- How can you make attitude your ally and not become overwhelmed with negativity, worry, anxiety, or worst-case scenarios?
- How can you empower, encourage, and lift others during tough times?
- How will building your killer instinct and mental toughness in advance of adversity help you to handle it more productively when you meet it?
- How can you take something terrible that has happened and weave it into your *WHY* to give you more to fight for?
- What else can you do to cause adversity to bring out the best in you, not the stress in you?

Chapter Two

THE *WHY* FUELS THE WAY

When it comes to achieving bigger goals, having clear and compelling internal motivators that fuel killer instinct and build mental toughness is a nonnegotiable. In this chapter, we will dive into why motivation is primarily an inside job and look at how to establish those personal motivators so that you are less dependent on external forces or other people for motivation. But first, consider the following breakdown of killer instinct's definition, because it establishes a foundation that we will build on throughout this chapter.

When you look at the definition of killer instinct, it talks about having an aggressive (attacking), tenacious (persistent) urge (strong feeling) for domination in a struggle to attain a goal. Bearing that in mind, it makes sense that the degree of killer instinct you possess is closely connected to the clarity and strength of your personal *WHY*.

This brings up three obvious questions:

1. What is a personal *WHY*?
2. How do I clarify my *WHY* and make it compelling?
3. How do I keep it clear and compelling throughout my life?

In the sixth chapter of my book *Unstoppable* (Wiley, 2017), "The Wonder of WHY," I explain the *WHY* in detail. Likewise, episode number eight of my *The Game Changer Life* podcast, "The Power of WHY," thoroughly covers this essential topic. While I won't duplicate those details here verbatim, I will lay out key points concerning the *WHY* to help put you on a firm footing in understanding this vital concept:

- Your *WHY* must specifically answer two questions: "Why do you get up each day?" and "Why should anyone else care that you get up each day?" In other words, *what* do you want for yourself, and *who* is counting on you to come through? The more specific and compelling your answers are to those questions, the stronger your *WHY* will be.
- Your *WHY* is personal. There is not a right or wrong *WHY*—just your *WHY*.
- Aspects of your *WHY* will change throughout your life.
- Your *WHY* comprises your most bold and compelling reasons for why you do what you do. People with strong reasons are less likely to let up, give up, lose focus and enthusiasm, or be negative as often or for as long. They simply cannot afford to be. Their reasons are so compelling that they don't give themselves those options.
- Your *WHY* is more than a goal or goals. It is a compilation of the *whys behind the WHY*—all the reasons why you want that goal or goals.

It is not just the $1 million annual income; it is what you will do with the million bucks: where you will live, what you will drive, how that will feel, who you will help, where you will send your kids to school, which debts you will retire, what new freedoms and options will be available to you, and the like.

The initial *WHY* goal—for example, the $1 million annual income—is rarely enough to keep you powering through significant sacrifices, setbacks, or disappointments by itself. It is *all the reasons why you want the goal* that fully ignites killer instinct, builds mental toughness, and makes you unstoppable.

You can download a free copy of our *WHY* booklet that walks you through the steps to carefully and specifically identify and articulate your *WHY* in the Insider Club at LearnToLead.com, and likewise listen to the corresponding *The Game Changer Life* podcast episode that runs approximately twenty minutes.

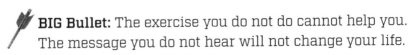

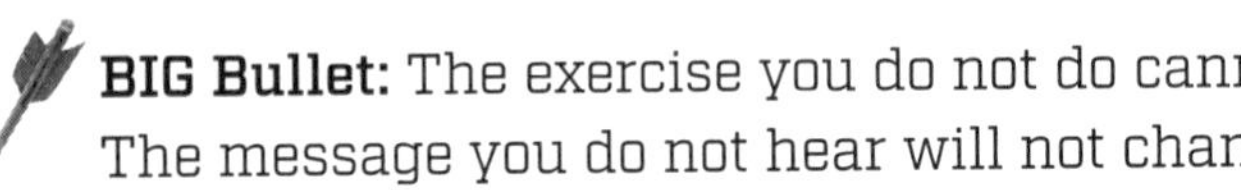

BIG Bullet: The exercise you do not do cannot help you.
The message you do not hear will not change your life.

To help demonstrate how one's *WHY* can influence performance among people performing identical duties, spend more time with Fred, Frank, and Frances, the three coworkers introduced in chapter one who will be your companions throughout the various chapters and lessons in this book—and explore the disparities in their success. Keep in mind, the three of them are part of a ten-person sales team and have had the same training, sell the same product, and work the same shift, with the option to put in additional time if they are behind in their sales goals. They also share the same manager, Alex. Fred has two years in with the company; Frank is the senior member, recently celebrating a decade with the organization; and Frances is the junior member of the three, having been with the company eighteen months.

You will undoubtedly enjoy the company of some of the three more than others, but each one offers much to teach. You are likely to see certain aspects of yourself in each of the three (perhaps identifying more with one than the others), gain inspiration and knowledge from aspects of each's performance, and learn what not to do from other tendencies they demonstrate in their thinking and behaviors.

FRED

In terms of performance, it appears that Fred may have peaked in high school. The competitiveness and work ethic he put into football positioned him for scholarship offers from multiple Division I institutions, right up until he blew out his knee in practice. Disheartened, he still enrolled in college without scholarships but dropped out during his sophomore year, after his high school sweetheart dumped him. In retrospect, it looks like she made a good choice.

Throughout his twenties, Fred worked multiple jobs including construction, security guard, driving a bread truck, and selling insurance. Despite his firm's extensive training and the investment they have made in him over his two years of employment, the quality and quantity of Fred's work is routinely substandard. He requires extensive external motivation to perform at mere average levels. Every once in a while, he surpasses expectations (showing what he can do if and when he puts his mind to it) only to quickly fall back into his old performance patterns.

Unfortunately, but not uncommon with lower performers like himself, Fred has built a lifestyle his mediocre career can support financially and seems content just to have a sales job with a nationally known franchise. He is perpetually complacent: satisfied that he is doing "okay" and even better than some people in his family and friendship circles. Fred compares himself against the two sales reps on his team who routinely produce less than him—rather than measuring and evaluating his results against where he should be based on his own potential—and comforts himself in saying, "At least I'm not the guy at the bottom."

Like so many people, Fred's *WHY* in life is unclear and/or uninspiring. It lacks aspirations that would cause him to change, work harder, become more consistent, or improve his skills. He has a "just enough" *WHY* that allows him to do just enough to get by, just enough to get paid, and just enough to not get fired. Fred has minimal drive and a killer instinct that normally only manifests at breaks, lunch hours, and quitting time. Whatever mental toughness he had as a high school football star was apparently blown out right along with his knee.

While he routinely blames his own bad luck, "flaky" customers, or an incompetent manager for lackluster performance—and often laments that his more successful teammates get more breaks—Fred is his own worst enemy. His indifferent and negative outlook on life marginalizes his two years of experience and vast knowledge of his products and processes. His tendency to make excuses and blame conditions he cannot control creates a victim's mindset that routinely leaves him unhappy, unfocused, and unfulfilled. Despite the tough state he has put himself in, his current mediocre performance status is not a permanent verdict unless he allows it to be. He mentally and emotionally "quit" the company long ago but will stay there physically as long as management tolerates, which buys him time to evaluate his next move. Rather than a change of scene, it is a change of self he needs, but it is not going to happen in the moving van on his way to the next career stop. He could change his life by changing his thinking, but up until now that prospect is scarier than the mediocrity and misery he has mastered and learned to live with.

FRANK

Frank is more motivated and ambitious than Fred. His father, a high-profile defense attorney, was hard on him growing up, set high expectations for his academics, and held him accountable throughout his childhood. Unfortunately, regardless of what Frank did in school—the sports he played, the girls he dated, the friends he chose, you name it—nothing was ever good enough for Frank Sr. The chip that Junior carries around on his shoulder to prove his dad's claim wrong that he would never amount to much drives him hard. Frank comes to work ready to make something happen and follows prescribed sales processes with every customer, giving total effort to make the sale. If he doesn't make the sale, though, he rarely follows up with that customer, and instead focuses on getting a fresh customer and opportunity. After all, his mindset is that he needs to make something happen *today* and that tomorrow can fend for itself.

Because his *WHY* is clearer and more compelling, Frank is normally among the top three salespeople on his ten-person team. He has a goal board on a wall in his home that has the car, the house, and the watch he wants to own. He longs for the day he will live in *that* house and drive *that* car wearing *that* watch to visit his folks. However, Frank has a level of drive that, while better than most individuals, has not graduated to consistent killer instinct yet, and his marginal mental toughness is manifest in how quickly he gives up on a customer he was unable to sell, opting to focus instead on a new customer he hopes is easier.

While he is performing at higher levels and doing so more consistently than Fred, Frank still becomes complacent after big wins and allows prosperity to drain his urgency. For example, he scored a personal best sales month in March, only to let up and struggle near the middle of the pack in April and May before returning to form in June. With the customer base he has built over the past decade, he should be vying for top of the sales board each month. But Frank is stuck in his ways. He became a know-it-all after one year in the business and has repeated that same experience over again the past nine years, learning and applying little that is new or more effective.

Frank's managers hope that his recent marriage and new daughter broadens his *WHY* for becoming more successful and consistent—beyond simply earning his dad's respect and his material goals—and validates their belief that Frank has superstar ability within him, and that with some minor adjustments in focus, attitude, work ethic, teachability, and consistency, this untapped potential of his will be drawn out in the near future.

FRANCES

Frances is a twice-divorced recovering alcoholic, who has been sober since her special-needs daughter, Amy, was born seven years ago. She is also a killer in sales. Like Frank, she gets to work ready to go and gives her all to each customer who walks through the doors. But unlike Frank, Frances does not wait for opportunities to come to her; she is always prospecting for new business, giving out her cards to people she meets throughout the course of her everyday interactions as she stops for coffee, gas, and groceries.

Frances has a level of drive that has advanced to killer instinct. Whereas "drive" is defined as "an innate biologically determined urge to attain a goal or satisfy a need," killer instinct speaks of the aggressive (attacking), tenacious (persistent) urge.[11] While being "driven" is necessary and foundational for greater success, killer instinct is a higher degree of drive; it is like drive on steroids. To supplement her killer instinct, Frances is also very mentally tough. She tries skillfully and persistently to make the sale today, and if the customer leaves without purchasing, she will stay in contact and build her relationship over time until the customer "buys or dies."

Frances is steered by a potent *WHY* composed of multiple factors, but three are primary:

- She works hard to prove wrong those in her family of academics who dismissed her sales job as "not a real career."
- She is motivated to silence with her success male coworkers who routinely disrespect and talk down to her as the sole woman on the team of ten.
- However, the most compelling aspect of Frances's *WHY* is Amy, who requires specialized and expensive schooling, day care, and medical treatments. Her house still needs additions to accommodate

> Amy's condition, and she is saving to buy a customized van that will make transporting Amy easier. Frances also enjoys investing in a professional wardrobe that reinforces her accomplished and successful image.

Frances's reasons for making sales each day are so strong that she cannot allow herself the luxury of engaging in trivial conversations with unproductive team members, making excuses or blaming, or wasting any time in low-return tasks at work. Because of her laser focus, she is wrongly considered aloof, selfish, and conceited by coworkers. Frances, however, couldn't care less what others misguidedly think of her. She has been the top salesperson on her team for fifteen straight months and, in her view, the others could better spend their time emulating her example rather than taking shots at her. In fact, their pettiness and idiocy are compelling aspects of her *WHY*; there is *no* way she would let any of them beat her out for the number one salesperson position. Despite her drive to win, she is a team player; the team just does not seem to want her help—primarily because it is *her* help.

Quality time away from work spent with Amy is a priority for Frances, and so she consistently works hard and smart so that she does not have to work the optional extra hours to surpass her objectives like many of her underperforming teammates do each month. Frances intentionally builds and reinforces the right mindset each morning by reviewing her written *WHY*, affirmations, and daily priorities, making sure to avoid negative morning news shows and to instead listen to a motivational podcast over coffee before leaving for work, and another while driving to work. By the time she walks into the workplace she is already focused, energized, in her zone, and ready to attack the day. While she is still human and prone to get off track from time to time, her reasons—her *WHY*—do not allow complacency to encroach in her life as often or for as long as Fred, Frank, or the others on her team.

BE A FRANCES, NOT A FRED

Once your *WHY* is clearly defined, compelling, relevant, and reviewed daily like it is with Frances, developing and strengthening the key ACCREDITED traits (attitude, competitiveness, character, rigor, effort, discipline, intelligence, tenacity, energy, and drive) becomes a natural and consistent consequence of right thinking, effort, and resolve. As long as it is unclear, uncompelling, or incomplete like Fred's or Frank's, expect to be *interested* in getting better and doing better at what you do, but in also being *committed* to little that is different or new in order to make that happen—drifting here and there looking for a quicker, easier way to get what you want most in life, and prone to whipping out your black belt in blame when you fall short.

BIG Bullet: Interested people are *curious* about something. Committed people *pledge* themselves to something. Two different things, lives, and legacies.

Developing killer instinct is as much about deciding what you want—your *WHY*—as it is about eliminating the unproductive and trivial activities prone to douse your inner fire. The problem for most folks is that because they never get clear enough about what they absolutely must say *yes* to every day to achieve what they want most, they have no idea what to say *no* to, what to avoid, or what to spend less time with, which we will discuss in depth in chapter ten. But once you have clearly defined your *WHY*, then both what you absolutely must do and what you must routinely reject, both day in and day out, become abundantly clear.

This principle explains why Frances, powered by her intentional mindset, goes to work to *work*, rather than engage in the ubiquitous "garbage" conversations about politics or sports, complain about management, and more that pop up throughout the day, nickel and diming away the time and productivity of each unfocused partaker. She doesn't care that others criticize her for not being "one of the guys." What matters to her is getting what she wants most in life, and to that end she would much rather be alone and productive than popular and in miserable or mediocre company.

Because Fred's *WHY* is either unclear or uninspiring, he gives himself too many unproductive options and routinely engages in them too often and for too long.

As for Frank, since his *WHY* steels his focus and energy to more consistent levels of productive thinking and activities, he is less likely to get off track as frequently or for as long as Fred. As his *WHY* becomes clearer and more captivating, so too will his ability to make intentional decisions regarding his time: steering his focus to spend it on the daily activities and associations that align with his goals, while avoiding the nonsense that knocks him off track.

BIG Bullet: Developing more compelling killer instinct is an inside job. No one can give it to you, put it in you, or do it for you. Whatever its level in your life, you own it.

WHERE THERE'S A *WHY*, THERE'S A WAY

Your daily focus, decision-making filters, downtime activities, and prioritized workplace activities all stem from your *WHY*. Your work ethic, character choices, resilience to bounce back from disappointments, and will to persist and power through adversity are all supported by a *WHY* that leaves you only one choice: to fight on. Your discipline, internal motivation, the habits you start or break, the people you leave, or the new friends you make are all influenced by the clarity and compelling force of your *WHY*. It all starts with *WHY*.

This is the reason that the renowned "Red Belt Mindset" principle, based on the martial arts, is so applicable to staying hungry in all aspects of life. In many martial arts disciplines, a red belt is the rank immediately preceding the coveted black belt. Having pursued the black belt rank for years, and investing time, effort, and energies to hone his or her technique, a practitioner with a red belt is so close to their goal that their *WHY* drives them to work harder, persist longer, and to stay hungry and humble because they have not yet "arrived." They still have so much worth fighting for. The black belt, on the other hand, is prone to taking a mental exhale once achieving his or her rank—their *WHY* just got smaller—and over time is less likely to work as hard or be as teachable or as humble as the hungry red belt. Increasing killer instinct and mental toughness requires you to continue to think like a red belt, even if you are a tenth-degree grand master.

Though the Red Belt Mindset principle has its roots in the martial arts, it has a much broader application to all of life's arenas: With reasons compelling enough to fight and change for, you can become unstoppable. Without them, or until you have ones that are compelling enough to create an intentional mindset, build mental toughness, and develop a killer instinct, you will not put in the time, go to the trouble, or disrupt the status quo you have learned to live with, and you are likely to plateau quickly and eventually decline. Again, it all starts with *WHY*.

Where there's a *WHY*, there is hope, energy, dreams, and power. Where there is a *WHY*—your personal and powerful *WHY*—there is a way. You will find it, or it may find you, but your daily journey in pursuit of *WHY* will create a collision course with you: one that you never knew existed and wish you had met sooner.

INTENTIONAL ACTION

Be intentional and visit the Insider Club at LearnToLead.com and download and then complete the *WHY* booklet. Listen to episode eight of *The Game Changer Life* podcast, "The Power of *WHY*." Take the time, as you work through the booklet's exercises, to create resolute clarity as to why you get up each day and why anyone else should care that you get up each day. When articulating your *WHY*, lean heavily on the whys behind the *WHY*: all the reasons you want the goals that comprise your *WHY*. *This* is the foundation for fueling a more intentional mindset that steers you away from what is unproductive and toward what is essential.

Refer to the areas of your life you identified as being complacent in the previous chapter and confirm that the *WHY* you have created is specific and compelling enough to force complacency in these areas from your life.

BADGERS ADVERSITY INCIDENT #2

June 24, 2019: Coach Moore Heart Attack

In the last chapter, I relayed the Howard Moore family tragedy incident. A short month later, tragedy struck again before the team's season even began.

Roughly one month after the tragic Coach Moore family accident, the entire team and staff were able to visit Coach Moore at his home for the first time. Coach Moore was standing, and he greeted the team with his familiar beaming smile, warmth, and strength. After being initially shaken on seeing his extensive burn damage and bandaging, the team circled around their coach in his living room as he described the accident and its aftermath:

- His son, Jerrell, had saved his life by dragging him from the burning wreckage despite his own injuries.
- The adversity had created a crossroads for Coach Moore in that he realized the incident could cause him either to run away from his strong Christian faith or run closer to it, and he had chosen the latter.
- The accident had caused him to resolve to become a better man, coach, friend, and neighbor, and to be the best he could in each of those roles. Coach Moore went around the room and challenged each man by name to become better in specific duties related to their own role as well. "Micah, you need to be the best rebounder it's possible for you to be. Brad, your role is to be the strongest leader you can possibly be. Meech, you're going to become the best point guard you can be."
- Moore discussed the obstacles he still faced on the road to recovery and explained how the team would meet their own obstacles in the upcoming season, still months away, and would need to fight through them as well.

The team left that night buoyed by their coach's positivity and strength. They looked forward to having him back coaching them at some point during the season and were finally able to focus on maximizing their off-season to prepare for the 2019–2020 schedule.

Just days after the team visited Coach Moore, he suffered a heart attack brought on by blood clot complications, and he slipped back into a coma.

PLAY A POOR HAND WELL

When tragedy strikes you or those you care about:

- How can you lift them as Coach Moore lifted his team, despite your own personal tragedies and challenges?
- How can you lift others in your family, team, or workplace to help them gain perspective and focus on the next right thing to do despite what is going on around you?
- How can you keep yourself focused and motivated in the midst of heartaches, disappointments, or loss?
- What else can you do to cause adversity to bring out the best in you, not the stress in you?

Chapter Three

MENTAL TOUGHNESS HELPS YOU FINISH!

Mental toughness is more than simply persisting toward a goal despite obstacles, setbacks, or disappointments; it also embodies the necessary resilience to recover quickly from losses or defeats throughout your journey. Some people have enough mental toughness to fight hard for what they want, but when they fall short or lose out, they take too long to regroup, recharge, and rebound, and oftentimes quit altogether. The good news is that like killer instinct, you can elevate your mental toughness intentionally, meaningfully, and consistently.

BIG Bullet: Attacking a goal is important but not enough. Persisting toward a goal is essential but incomplete. Rebounding quickly after setbacks or defeat is the ingredient missing in masses who become successful but never reach their potential.

Mental toughness is looked at as a measure of confidence and resilience predictive of success in education, athletics, or the workplace. The beauty of this two-part definition—confidence and resilience—is that once you build more confidence or belief in your abilities (which you can do intentionally), you will become more resilient because your belief in yourself is stronger.

THE UNCOMFORTABLE STRATEGY

If mental toughness is built on confidence and resilience, then the question becomes, how do you build more confidence and thus become more resilient in the process? Let's first talk about how you *don't* do it. For starters, you do not build confidence and resilience doing what you are comfortable with or what you have always or already done. While those things may maintain your current level of confidence and resilience—and naturally, if you stop doing them the confidence you currently have may diminish—to *build* confidence you have got to change, to stretch, to risk, and to extend yourself beyond what you have done before. You need to routinely behave in a manner that makes you uncomfortable, working diligently against the persistent pull of complacency to step out of your comfort zone, change, and stretch consistently across life's most vital sectors: work, relationships, finances, health, spirituality, and more.

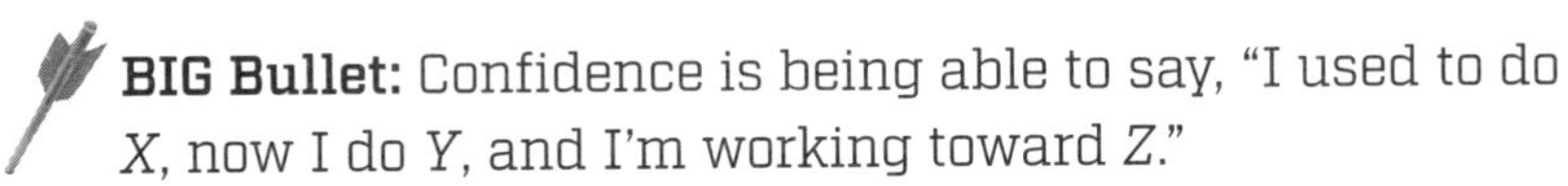

BIG Bullet: Confidence is being able to say, "I used to do *X*, now I do *Y*, and I'm working toward *Z*."

YOUR TWO SELFS

Incidentally, self-esteem and self-confidence are different. Self-esteem concerns belief in yourself as a good and worthy person. Self-confidence is about belief in your abilities. It is not uncommon to have larger amounts of one of these traits, and not the other. For example, you can have strong self-esteem and low self-confidence when performing a task for which you are ill-suited or untrained. On the other hand, you may have high confidence when performing a task at which you are proficient but possess low self-esteem because you do not see value in yourself as a person or in your work. For greater success and fulfillment, it is essential to have strong measures of both, and an intentional mindset will help you to purposefully build both of these critical success factors into your life.

SHE WILL, HE WON'T, AND SO-SO

When Frances first began prospecting during her weekly errands—letting people know who she was and what she did, giving out her business card, and gathering the prospect's contact information for follow-up—it was way out of her comfort zone. When she would later call to thank them for their time and invite them to stop by her store for coffee the next time they were in the neighborhood, it felt awkward. But she did it anyway because she was new in her position and she could not afford to sit around and wait on customers to walk through the door. She needed to create her own customers so she could attain the success that would satisfy her *WHY*. When she began to see the fruits of her efforts, she became more resolved—and confident—to stay the course and do what others in her business were not willing to do, and thus she achieved what they were unable to attain.

Like Frances, Fred tried prospecting outside the workplace and, as is to be expected with something new, he was clumsy with his words and approach. Needless to say, it made him very uncomfortable and when he did not get results right away, he gave up. His lack of confidence was obvious to his potential customers, and he never persisted long enough to refine his approach. This had been Fred's pattern for years: reluctantly try something new, soon thereafter flinch in the face of discomfort, and quit before he could develop proficiency or discipline. Over time, he believed less in himself and in his abilities and hunkered down in his comfort zone doing what he had always done and reaping what he had always gotten in the past, which was never much more than average.

Frank is good at prospecting with others he meets in his off-time but is only motivated to execute his skill when business is slow at the store and customers have stopped coming to him. His lack of killer instinct and mental toughness in this regard surrenders a significant edge to Frances in the monthly sales contests and is a primary culprit for his never once beating her out for salesperson of the month.

BIG Bullet: When your *WHY* is big enough, you won't give yourself the option to *not* do what you know you should do just because you dislike it or don't feel like doing it.

CHANGE YOUR BASIS

An effective method for building mental toughness is to continually look for ways to "change your basis." Your basis is whatever you are currently doing as part of your personal, workout, or work routine that you have mastered and with which you are comfortable. It may be productive, but it does not challenge you like it once did because you are used to it. For instance, attaining a goal to read one book per month, or visit the gym three times per week, may have been tough when you first started, but after time you are nearly 100 percent consistent month in and month out. Your basis in those areas are ideal candidates to take the confidence you have already built there, raise it, and make yourself temporarily uncomfortable. Doing so constructs a higher level of confidence and resilience because you have disrupted your comfortable routine and are increasing your performance. Raising your basis is even more effective if you apply the principle incrementally and consistently, in multiple areas of your life, simultaneously.

For instance, Frank averages ten follow-up or prospecting calls per day, which is better than the team average of eight. Frank consistently executes this discipline and has successfully figured out how to fit it into his daily routine, regardless of how busy he is with other matters. Ten quality phone calls a day is his consistent basis. The downside with continuing in this discipline is that it is comfortable for Frank. It is *no longer a challenge*, and that is why his mental toughness will not increase. By making his ten daily calls he is certainly *maintaining* the level of confidence and resilience he is at currently, but until he raises his basis, he will not see an *increase* in his mental toughness.

If Frank decided to raise his basis to twelve quality calls per day, it might feel awkward at first. Likewise, he might be less consistent executing those calls until he figured out how to more productively structure his day and spend less time with unproductive tasks to free up time to make the additional calls. But, as he worked through that initial discomfort, he could soon master his new routine and as a result would have upped this productive activity by 20 percent daily, raising his basis, his sights, his confidence, and his results. Within a reasonable period of time he could repeat the process and go from twelve to fourteen, from fourteen to fifteen, and so forth. Since confidence is rooted in "belief in one's abilities," his confidence, along with the resilience it fuels, would steadily rise as he consistently accomplished what he had not done previously. The result? More mental toughness, built intentionally, over time.

BIG Bullet: Consider your basis as a rest stop, not a rest home.

GET COMFORTABLE BEING UNCOMFORTABLE

Here is where mental toughness really compounds. If, while he was raising his basis at work, Frank also increased his nightly routine of five sets of ten push-ups to five sets of twelve push-ups, and upped his monthly discipline of reading one book per month to one-and-one-half books per month, he could begin to steadily and intentionally transform his mental toughness and results at a pace that would consistently grow and evolve into exponentially new levels in due time. By increasing his basis across multiple life arenas simultaneously, incrementally, and consistently, Frank would develop a mentally tough mindset where he *became increasingly comfortable being uncomfortable*, which is a trait of top performers in any endeavor.

BIG Bullet: In the words of Jim Rohn, it's common to want to get more without first becoming more and doing more, but "to get more than you've got you must first become more than you are and do more than you do."[12]

The bottom line though, is this: Until Frank's reasons for raising his basis, his *WHY*, are emboldened to a point that leaves him no choice but to elevate his effort, he will continue to find reasons why his current basis is fine as is, and take comfort in the fact that it is already much higher than someone like Fred's. The resistance to change his basis is even more likely since Frank tends to measure himself against others versus his own potential, and most of his team members make eight calls or less daily, his friends do not do any push-ups at all, and no one he knows well reads even one serious book per year, much less per month. Thus, Frank already feels so superior in these areas that he sees no need to extend himself further because he is basing "superiority" on being better than others rather than on being better than his former self.

BIG Bullet: The fact that your performance outshines others' does not testify to your own growth or potential to grow further—only that others are worse than you in certain areas.

While Frank provides our example here, the "I'm already better than him or her, so why work harder," dynamic just described is far from uncommon and demonstrates a complacent mindset that allows people who are doing well to become content with what they are doing because they compare themselves to what others are doing, rather than to what they *could* be doing. It all goes back to the stuck-in-his-ways, unteachable nature rooted in complacency that stops him from realizing his potential and truly becoming his best. Sadly, and typically, Frank is too often comfortable being comfortable because it "works" for him and makes him better than most. In his mind he asks, "Why do more?" and "What's all the fuss about?" If his *WHY* was compelling enough, he would bother, and he would understand what the fuss is all about. He could not *not* bother, and he would make a fuss. His reasons would let him do no less.

YOU'RE THE COMPETITION

This is a good time to revisit the definition of killer instinct and reinterpret it within the context of building an intentional mindset as it supports this point:

> Killer instinct: "an aggressive, tenacious urge to dominate in the quest to overcome a struggle or attain a goal."

Performers like Frank interpret this definition to mean that the struggle is to dominate another person. They view that the goal is to become better than others. Performers aspiring to build an intentional mindset so they can become intentionally great interpret the definition differently.

Their struggle is to dominate their *previous self*, the person they were formerly: the attitude they had; how competitive they were; yesterday's character choices, rigor, effort, discipline, intelligence, tenacity, energy, and drive. *That* is the goal for elite performers like Frances. *They* are their own competition.

BIG Bullet: When you continue to better your own best, you may very well become *the* best, but regardless, mastering others is subordinate to mastering oneself.

BE UNNATURAL

When *you* are your own biggest competition, not only does raising your basis come naturally, but remaining smugly comfortable with your routine is not even an option. Think of raising your basis and building mental toughness like building a muscle: through resistance, repetition, and by regularly adding weight (not so much weight at once that you will regress, but reasonable amounts of added weight, over time, until you have exponentially surpassed your former best performances). It all happens one incremental step forward at a time, in due course. The challenge here, though, is threefold:

- People crave comfort and *naturally* resist uncertainty, resistance, or change.
- People do not *naturally* develop the discipline or consistency to become repetitious with the activities that matter most; normally because they do not "feel" like doing them or are too unfocused or unstructured to do them.
- People do not *naturally* want to add "weight" and take on more than they are doing, because they are comfortable and confident with the weight they already know they can handle.

This is why it is essential to build an intentional mindset that seeks discomfort, embraces resistance, and enjoys adding weight so that doing what is *unnatural* for most people has become natural for you.

There is also an opportunity to build confidence and improve performance by lowering your basis of unproductive activities. For instance, if you are accustomed to watching three hours of television nightly, you could shave off thirty minutes and do something more productive with that time. This, too, would create discomfort as you disturb your comfort zone but has the same positive effect of raising your basis on confidence and mental toughness.

As a reminder regarding the previous chapter's Intentional Action section: Since the catalyst for changing your basis is having compelling enough reasons to change your basis, it is essential to define or clarify your *WHY* if you have not already. The chances are good that if you have lost your *WHY*, you have also lost your way, and you must take the time to reenergize your focus and energy by redefining it more clearly and compellingly.

BIG Bullet: A *WHY* is not just what you want to get but who you want to become. Once you become clear on your desired identity, making better decisions in accordance with that type of person is easier and more natural.

NOT EASY BUT WORTH IT

Even after you have become consistent at continually disrupting areas of your life (your basis) that seem to be working for you, or that are comfortable, certain, and safe, and it becomes part of your nature—it still is not going to be easy. It will, however, be worth it. That is precisely why it is important to build an intentional mindset: so that you do what is unnatural and what others are not willing to do to live a life you would have never been able to live—one others will not be able to live because they are tucked snugly into the certainty of their comfort zone.

INTENTIONAL ACTION

Consider at least three aspects of your various routines you are used to, that are productive, and that you do consistently. This could include various aspects of your work or exercise routines, personal growth regimen, and more. Simultaneously raise your basis in each of these areas to create the discomfort and build the mental toughness you need to become intentionally great. Also consider possible areas for lowering your basis of unproductive activities and replacing them with productive actions.

BADGERS ADVERSITY INCIDENT #3

November 5, 2019: Badgers Lose Season Opener in Overtime

As the team rallied around the Moore family and made the mental and personnel adjustments necessary to try to remain productive in his absence—and as his recovery uncertainty continued—they committed to getting the season off to a great start with a win against a nationally ranked opponent.

With Coach Moore's fate still uncertain, the Badgers dedicated the season to their stricken coach. They created and rallied around the motto, "Do Moore. Be Moore. 4 Moore."

The team was scheduled to play nationally ranked, number-twenty St. Mary's for the season opener at a neutral site, the Sanford Pentagon, in Sioux Falls, South Dakota. To honor Coach Moore and live out their new motto, the team visited children at the Sanford Children's Hospital in Sioux Falls before the game. In pre-game warm-ups the Badgers sported the newly created "Do Moore. Be Moore. 4 Moore" warm-up shirts—a tradition they would carry on the entire season. Both teams honored Coach Moore and his family with a moment of silence before the game. Despite holding the lead with time running out, the Badgers lost in overtime 65–63 to begin the year dedicated to Coach Moore with a record of 0–1.

PLAY A POOR HAND WELL

- What steps do you take, or can you take, to refocus following emotional letdowns or a series of letdowns that can create a form of mental devastation?
- Do you have a strategy for taking something that appears to happen *to* you and use it to happen *for* you? What is that strategy? What could it be going forward?
- What are potential benefits of fighting hard but coming up short or when you feel you have let someone down?

Chapter Four

DECISIONS DETERMINE DIRECTION

When Frances was brought back into the workplace after being furloughed during the COVID-19 pandemic, she was ready to produce. She was ready because she never got unready during her time away. Unlike Fred, who daily slept in and spent his time glued to the news or bouncing between two Netflix series he had acquired addictions to, Frances made better decisions and gained an edge.

- She *decided* to wake up at her normal time and exercise.
- She *decided* to update her *WHY* and reviewed it each morning during her intentional mindset routine.
- She *decided* to invest her downtime taking an online sales mastery course, reading one self-help book per month, and researching her competitor's products online.

Unfortunately, Fred's approach while furloughed set the stage for a regression in his already-mediocre performance after returning.

- Fred *decided* to focus on, and was obsessed by, the aspects of his life that he could not control: the ever-changing government mandates and news of the daily infection rate and death count tallies.
- Fred *decided* to spend more time on social media making repeat trips through the buffet of blame, and binge on the danger du jour, posting his frustrations and becoming involved in endless debates on his social channels.
- Fred *decided* to waste time speculating endlessly about when his stimulus check might arrive and what else the government might do to help him through the difficulties.

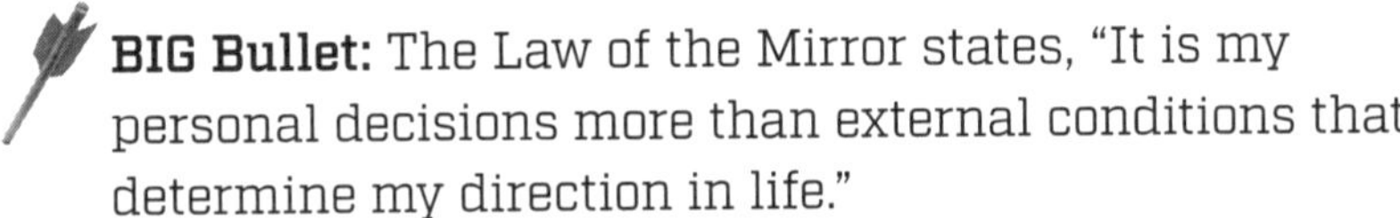

BIG Bullet: The Law of the Mirror states, "It is my personal decisions more than external conditions that determine my direction in life."

As is typical throughout mankind's history, people surrounded by identical conditions make vastly different decisions that determine, to drastic effect, different directions. In Fred's mind the pandemic happened *to* him, and as a result, he allowed a victim's thinking to immobilize him. Frances decided to find a way to use the pandemic to her advantage: to stay sharp, to learn new things, to up her game, and to gain an edge. Her better decisions made the crisis happen *for* her.

Intentionally building your mindset is at the core of leveraging the power of right decisions and relying less on favorable conditions to get ahead. It is the catalyst for living life more like the boxer than the bag: being proactive, setting the pace, and controlling the fight. This is not to say that tough conditions beyond your control have no effect on your life's trajectory, but simply that making the right decisions as you face those conditions can marginalize the impact. The fact is that wherever you are now in life is very much the result of decisions you have made, and the decisions you make each day forward greatly determine your future.

BIG Bullet: "Success isn't an accident, but an accumulation of right decisions and disciplines repeated over daily. Failure isn't an accident, but an accumulation of wrong decisions and disciplines repeated over daily."[13] —Jim Rohn

To illustrate how different people going through the same conditions can either build or diminish their killer instinct and mental toughness based on the decisions they make, let's look deeper at Fred, Frank, and Frances's decisions during the COVID-19 pandemic—when a government-mandated shutdown of nonessential businesses forced a ninety-day closure of their office—and after, when they returned from furlough. We will focus on two of the ACCREDITED traits as a basis for each person's outlook: attitude and tenacity.

A LITTLE DIFFERENCE THAT MAKES A BIG DIFFERENCE

Attitude is defined as "a settled way of thinking reflected in one's behavior; one's prevailing outlook on life."[14] An aspect of building an intentional mindset that develops mental toughness and a killer instinct is to manage your attitude and focus on the things you can control throughout your life, knowing that while you cannot regulate what happens to you, you are still responsible for how you respond to it.

BIG Bullet: Attitude is a choice. The quality of your response determines the quantity of your progress.

Fred used the COVID-19 crisis as an excuse to mentally check out of even trying to stay productive during his months of furlough, opting instead to live passively and wait to be rescued.

As a result of his decision to be victimized by the furlough, Fred lost ground in both killer instinct and mental toughness. Not only did he allow the modicum of drive that he had to be snuffed out by conditions beyond his control, he was not even able to maintain the confidence he once had, consequently causing him to become less resilient. He began to live reactively, more like the bag than the boxer: getting beat up and pushed around, and withdrawing rather than initiating. His attitude allowed no room for seeing how the furlough could possibly benefit him, and instead dwelled throughout the day on all that was happening to him.

Frank decided to use some downtime to read a second book each month, starting with one on goal setting, but could not keep his eyes off his nearby computer, where he was continually distracted by newsbreaks of business closures, soaring unemployment figures, updated government mandates, and stock market fluctuations. He never progressed past chapter one. Frank was unwilling to make a choice to put the distractions away and focus on reading. The message he missed within those pages could have changed his life.

Much like during the average workweek where he would begin each Monday with good intentions, Frank's unwillingness to make the choice to avoid what's trivial, negative, and beyond his control and focus instead on more productive tasks cost him growth in both killer instinct and mental toughness.

Frances, being a volleyball player in high school and an avid sports fan, considered the furlough as a sort of "off-season," and approached it in many ways as she would during her summers as a teenager: to gain an edge. Since she knew there would be much ground to make up for on her return, she decided to double down on the aspects of her life that she could control—especially how she used her schedule—and created a regimen that improved her attitude, skills, and knowledge. Her doubling down on staying structured and productive also revealed opportunities to improve that she had not even recognized before the crisis.

Despite her productivity overall while furloughed, Frances found it uncomfortable to face weaknesses in some of her downtime habits—namely, spending too much time following the presidential campaign on social media. This made her realize how often in the past she had failed to maximize both her time at work and home, primarily because she had convinced herself that her superior results were evidence she must be doing every productive thing possible. Thus, she had unconsciously stopped seeking ways to tweak her basis. But by acting on the discomfort of her discovery rather than dismissing it, she was able to convert her disgust into motivation to improve and started making better decisions in those regards. Faced with the same conditions as Fred and Frank, Frances looked reality dead in the eye and decided she had been her own biggest obstacle to being more productive, and she chose to get out of her own way by maximizing her limited and irreplaceable time.

BIG Bullet: You cannot fix what you do not face, nor change what you do not acknowledge.

PERSISTENCE TURBOCHARGED

Another of the ten ACCREDITED traits whose development is essential to augmenting both killer instinct and mental toughness is tenacity. Tenacity is defined as "the quality or fact of being very determined."[15] It's about persisting toward your goals even when it takes too long or feels too hard, after others who are chasing the same dreams as you have detoured, let up, or quit. In this way, tenacity is very much likened to turbocharged persistence. Tenacity, like attitude, is a choice.

When it was time to return to the workplace after the furlough period, Fred, Frank, and Frances once again differed, this time in their degrees of tenacity, when faced with the same opportunities and obstacles. Take note of how their tenacity differed, as well as how their decisions—when faced with identical conditions—either intensified or mitigated the levels of tenacity that were already part of their makeup. You may also wish to consider which of their responses you can most identify with in your own life.

BIG Bullet: Tenacity requires a decision. You don't get to choose the obstacles standing between you and your goals, but you can decide to relentlessly persist despite them.

Regardless of whether business is sluggish or robust, Frances works tenaciously toward the goals that comprise her *WHY*; the weightiness of those goals leaves her no choice. She does not have to be externally motivated, cajoled, guilted, begged, threatened, or bribed by others to consistently follow prescribed processes, smartly structure her daily routine, stay in touch with customers, or rebound from down days. She has embraced these disciplines for so long she does them without thinking. If an obstacle arises, it may break her stride temporarily, but it does not change her direction.

Tenacity has become one of Frances's defining characteristics—part of her makeup—and is a habitual pattern of behavior and a way of life that is natural for her. It can be the same for everyone who gets intentionally clear enough about achieving their *WHY*, focuses on it daily, and conditions themselves to do whatever it takes to achieve it.

BIG Bullet: You have got to have something worth fighting for before you are determined enough to stay in the fight. That "something" or "somethings" are the reasons comprising your *WHY*.

When Frank is having a tough month, he puts his game face on and doubles down on tenacity. He focuses like a laser on maximizing each day and the opportunities it brings. He boasts that he works best under pressure and when coming from behind, and he prides himself on fast finishes to a month after others have written him off.

Frank suffers from situational tenacity. He is very determined to become more successful when he is struggling, but once he is back on track, he relaxes. His lack of sufficient killer instinct and mental toughness allows temporary prosperity to produce only momentary urgency. *If only* Frank had stronger reasons for not letting up, he could contend with Frances each month for the top of the performance board. *If only* there was something more compelling he wanted. *If only* there were others or a cause beyond himself he was more committed to impact. *If only* he was on fire to become a better teammate and positively impact the team. *If only* is becoming the story of Frank's career and life. The straight-talk truth is this: *If only* Frank's *WHY* were more significant, he would stop giving life all that he had only when necessary and take his life to an entirely different level.

BIG Bullet: "On the Plains of Hesitation bleach the bones of countless millions who, at the Dawn of Victory, sat down to wait, and waiting—died!"[16] —George W. Cecil

Replace the "bleached bones" in that poignant quote with "potential," and you will understand the self-imposed fate of Frank and countless like him. It is important to remember that the "sat down to wait" component is not a condition, but a decision: *deciding* to let up, *deciding* to rest, *deciding* to mentally or physically check out, *deciding* to just quit outright. All are decisions; none are conditions. And wrong decisions create self-inflicted conditions that rob you of your best life.

Fred is primarily tenacious about two things in his life: remaining comfortable and explaining away why he is not more successful. In these arenas he is very determined, capable, and practiced. Fred has consistently invested his tenacity into these two objectives for so long he has become convinced he is right and that the universe is guilty of wrongly conspiring against both his comfort zone and perpetual embrace of victimhood.

BIG Bullet: The more often you engage in wrong thinking and behaviors, the more the unproductive things you think and do seem normal, and the less conscious you become of the consequences they inflict.

Just as ACCREDITED traits like energy and effort are only helpful if you apply them in the right measure (*well-invested* energy and *complete* effort), tenacity can work against you when you are very determined not to change, to resist discomfort, and to always be right. This issue clarifies why an ACCREDITED trait like "character" is so essential to killer instinct and mental toughness: It compels you to remain humble, stay teachable, accept responsibility, and hold yourself accountable for making the right decisions and executing effective disciplines. It is important to note here that in one way or another, each of the ten ACCREDITED traits impacts the others for better or worse as you strengthen or abuse them with your thinking and behaviors. After you have finished the book, you will have the opportunity to work for seventy days building an intentional mindset, investing time to improve traits like attitude and tenacity.

There is no way around it: Making the right decisions is the foundation of building an intentional mindset to improve mental toughness and develop a killer instinct. For example, you must *decide*:

- to get clear and compelling concerning your *WHY.*
- to engage in the daily activities that take you there.
- to minimize your time with, or avoid altogether, the activities that make it harder to get there.

- to change your basis.
- to become comfortable being uncomfortable.
- to do what is essential even if you do not like doing it.
- to do what is essential even though you may not feel like doing it.
- to focus more on the aspects of your life you can control and stop giving energy and attention to the things you cannot.
- to work on building your mindset with the same intentionality you build a healthy body.
- to associate with people who elevate you, not devastate you.
- to attack your goals.
- to fight to the finish.
- to remain humble and teachable throughout your journey.
- to do the Intentional Action exercises at the end of each chapter.
- to take the ACCREDITED course following the completion of this book.
- to apply what you learn from the lessons with both excellence and consistency.
- to decide more wisely and in alignment with all aspects of your *WHY* day in and day out.

Regardless the conditions you may yet face throughout the rest of your career or life, making decisions like those just listed will position you to prosper despite them.

BIG Bullet: Greater success is not about what you are capable of but what you are willing to do. You have got to close the gap between knowing and doing by embracing the reality that the right decisions done repeatedly compound success.

THE LAW OF THE MIRROR

As mentioned previously, The Law of the Mirror says, “It is my personal decisions more than external conditions that determine my direction in life.”

Building an intentional mindset where you take personal responsibility and focus more on making the productive decisions you can control, rather than becoming immobilized or victimized by what is beyond your control, creates a personal power unknown to life's championship whiners and victims: those who invest more energy into searching for scapegoats than solutions. Looking in the mirror helps build mental toughness because sometimes you do not like what you see or it makes you uncomfortable, but as you work to change that unhappy reality, your confidence grows, your killer instinct to be more and do more heightens, and you can become unstoppable.

INTENTIONAL ACTION

Write down aspects of your life concerning health, marriage, raising kids, relationships, work, or finances where you are disappointed with your current status or results. What is at least one specific and time-based decision you can make in each area to begin moving in a better direction and improve your success and fulfillment in that area?

BADGERS ADVERSITY INCIDENT #4

November 21, 2019: Micah Potter Ruled Ineligible for Another Month

After the Badgers' slow start to the season they had dedicated to Coach Moore, they counted especially on the eligibility of transfer student Micah Potter to help them pick up steam the remainder of November and December.

Micah Potter was an Ohio State University transfer who sat out the entire prior season, awaiting NCAA eligibility to play. Micah had followed all rules and protocols, and the Badgers looked forward to using his size and experience to fill the role they had for him and help get the season in gear.

After previously having his eligibility waiver denied, there was hope that a new hearing would right the apparent injustice. At a hearing on November 21, 2019, the NCAA, to the shock and dismay of all involved, delayed his eligibility another full month. He would not start his first game until December 21, 2019, missing roughly a third of the season. When the team most needed a big-bodied boost to give them an edge, forces beyond their control dashed their dream. The team would continue to miss his energy and abilities, persisting but feeling limited and short-handed without Micah on the court. Micah posted the following message on his Twitter account that day:

> My eligibility waiver was denied again today and sadly we now have closure. I'm extremely disappointed and frustrated that we've reached this point. I'm still confused why I am being punished for behaving in a manner that the NCAA requests of its student-athletes.
>
> For the next month, my goal continues to be what it has been, of doing everything possible to prepare my teammates for upcoming games and supporting them from the sidelines.
>
> I want to thank everybody that has helped me through this process and supported me, specifically Katie Smith, Scott

Tompsett, Barry Alvarez and certainly my coaching staff, teammates and family.

My faith has been my stronghold throughout this whole process and I know God has His perfect plan for everything.

I have no regrets and I'm proud to be a Badger and can't wait to compete in exactly one month.

On, Wisconsin![17]

PLAY A POOR HAND WELL

- How can you improve your response to adversities caused by injustices or other forces beyond your control?
- How can you encourage the person being persecuted?
- Did you ever have an injustice you initially thought was happening *to* you actually happen *for* you after time had passed and you reflected on the series of events?

Chapter Five

ATTITUDE

Build a Stronger ABLE So You're Able to Go Stronger

ABLE IS A BIG DEAL

While working with the Wisconsin Badgers men's basketball team, I introduced an acronym, ABLE, which represents attitude, body language, and energy. The thrust of ABLE is that attitude influences body language, and body language impacts energy levels. It all starts with attitude, "a settled way of thinking reflected in one's behaviors; one's prevailing outlook on life."[18]

Oftentimes you can see attitude in someone's behavior based on their body language and energy levels, long before you hear them speak. For instance, if a player missed multiple shots in a row, you could observe his head drop down or nod back and forth, shoulders slump, a sluggish pace in transition, and more—the human equivalent of Eeyore the donkey. The poor body language and low energy levels all started with the wrong thinking reflected in the player's attitude. Without adjusting his attitude, before long, this player might stop shooting altogether or shoot with minimal expectation that the ball even goes in.

Another player could miss the same five shots and yet appear unfazed, pick up his energy level, and shoot again as soon as he had the opportunity—believing he had gotten the kinks worked out with his series of misses and was due for a basket. Again, this is all based on the player's thinking: his attitude. It is his attitude that plays a significant role in influencing whether his levels of killer instinct and mental toughness will get him through the tough stretch or will cause him to crumble.

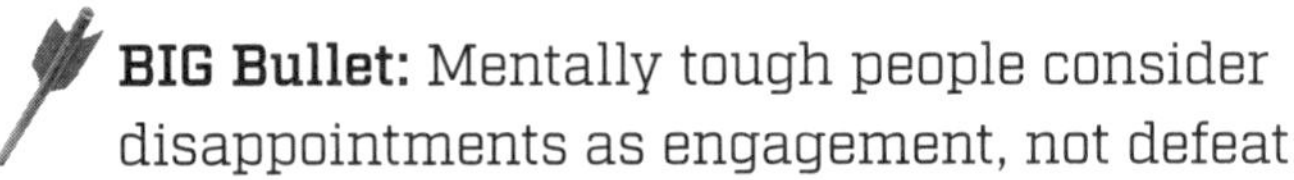

BIG Bullet: Mentally tough people consider disappointments as engagement, not defeat.

This illustration can be seen played out in education, athletics, and workplaces throughout the centuries: People with similar skills, knowledge, talent, and experience go through identical trials but choose to handle it in a completely different manner. This is why attitude is one of the ten ACCREDITED traits we will focus on in the book (and as you work through the follow-up course at its conclusion) and is a great place to begin: a healthy attitude is a *very* big deal.

When you later take the ACCREDITED follow-up course and daily evaluate and grade yourself on the seven aspects of attitude presented in this chapter, you will do so within the context of how you performed with attitude in all of life's arenas: at home or work; with friends, family, and strangers; during your workout; driving in traffic; waiting in line for groceries; watching your kid's softball game; and the like.

As you work in a similar fashion through the remaining ACCREDITED traits in the next chapters, you may notice that aspects of some traits are similar, identical, or seem to overlap. For instance, one aspect of rigor you will later be asked to evaluate is, "I successfully execute my daily priorities." Similarly, an aspect of effort will be, "I execute the most essential tasks." When you recognize similar or identical aspects recurring across multiple ACCREDITED traits, they deserve greater attention and diligence, because this repetition marks them as being especially important to developing a killer instinct and building mental toughness.

SEVEN KEY ASPECTS OF ATTITUDE

1. I RESPOND WELL TO NEGATIVE THINGS.

Fred and Frances each had a customer they had been working with decide to buy from a competitor. Upon this finding, Fred called a "fellowship of the miserable" meeting and shared the bad news with every coworker that would listen. He dismissed his customer as being a timewaster and remarked that if this was a sign of things to come, everyone was going to be in for a tough month. To the new associate on the team he mentioned, "You sure picked a tough time to join the industry. Hope your kids don't eat too much. May want to keep that resume up to date—this used to be a good place to work, but now I'm not so sure."

Frances, on the other hand, while discovering during her follow-up phone call that her customer had bought elsewhere, thanked the gentleman for his time, wished him well with his new purchase, and suggested that she would love another opportunity to serve him in the future. She then mentally replayed the entire encounter with the customer through her mind, looking for lessons (things she could have done better or a buying sign she might have missed), and determined she may not have spent enough time with the customer qualifying him on a product that best fit his needs, causing him to buy something he thought would better fit his needs elsewhere. She resolved to make a conscious effort to ask more questions about the next customer's buying motives so she could improve her chances of selecting the best solution for them. In her mind, this lost sale would help her improve her skills and make her many new sales as she refocused more on this important technique going forward.

BIG Bullet: "There is little difference in people, but the little difference makes a big difference. The little difference is attitude. The big difference is whether it is positive or negative."[19] —W. Clement Stone

BIG Question: Do you react too quickly to negative things, or take a few seconds to consider a more productive response, including a way to possibly benefit?

2. I AM NOT EASILY OFFENDED.

This aspect relates to numerous possible instances that can potentially impact your attitude and get you off track if you let them:

- something you see or read on social media
- something someone says about you that you interpret as demeaning or disrespectful
- when someone cuts you off in traffic
- feeling that you did not get enough credit for a job well done
- a joke you hear; a viewpoint contrary to yours; the tone in which someone addresses you; the server taking too long to refill your drink; someone bumping into you without saying "excuse me"; a lunchmate doing all the talking and not letting you get a word in; someone interrupting you mid-sentence; a teammate failing to say "thank you"; your spouse not saying "please"; and the like

All of these instances may give you legitimate reason to take offense, but your attitude will determine if you take the bait and shift your focus and energy to what is unproductive, or regard the incident as not mattering enough to invite misery into your life by repeating it, responding to it improperly, avenging it, or dwelling on it. No one suggests you become a doormat but rather that you should be discerning and choose your mental battles wisely. Within the context of reaching your potential as a human being, did what just happened really matter enough to give energy to it and invest irreplaceable time into it?

Frankly, people driven by a compelling *WHY*, who have developed the confidence and security of robust mental toughness, do not have time for life's nonsense that would distract them, drain them, or disable their ABLE. They are too focused on the big things to allow any little offenses on the way to slow them down, dilute their focus, drain their energy, or ding their attitude.

BIG Bullet: No one can offend you without your consent. The art of being wise is in knowing what, and whom, to overlook.

BIG Questions: Are you overly sensitive to things or people that, in the scope of reaching your potential as a human being, don't really matter that much? Do you too readily engage in things, or with people, that get you off track and make it harder to reach your goals?

3. I DEMONSTRATE POSITIVE SPEECH.

This aspect covers a lot of ground:

- focusing on solutions rather than just pointing out problems
- encouraging or complimenting others
- speaking well of those not present
- refraining from gossip, complaining, or speculating over worst-case scenarios
- avoiding off-color language and jokes; not expressing prejudices or judgments about others

Falling into any of the traps or similar behaviors listed above cheapens your presence, disables your ABLE, creates unproductive distractions for others, wastes energy on activities with no positive return, and douses your killer instinct. Additionally, reflecting on these behaviors later can make you feel worse about yourself, injuring your self-esteem, self-confidence, and the mental toughness that accompanies them. Words matter. A lot. This is because what comes out of your mouth is merely an extension of how and what you think in your mind and feel in your heart. It requires discipline (self-control) to wisely manage your words, and you are more inclined to do so when the stakes are higher: when considering if what you are about to say will move you closer to your *WHY* or make it more difficult to achieve it.

BIG Bullet: Words can inspire. And words can destroy. Choose yours well.

BIG Questions: Do your words mostly add energy and life to situations or take energy from them? Do they attract people and opportunities to you or repel them from you?

4. I FOCUS ON WHAT I CAN CONTROL.

Focus concerns the ability to concentrate.[20] Everyone focuses on something throughout the day, and what they are focusing on greatly determines whether they do the things that move them toward their *WHY* or make the path there tougher and longer than it should be.

Throughout the day it is important to guard your mind and speech against focusing on matters you cannot control because they can make you feel powerless and cause you to become passive. Passivity impairs ABLE, killer instinct, and mental toughness, and shifts commitment from working for your *WHY* to waiting it out.

Be informed about world events, but not obsessed to where they dominate your thinking and conversations. Do not talk negatively about other people or departments within your organization; instead, go talk to those people whenever possible. Avoid lamenting the customers, inventory, or resources you do not have and commit to maximizing what you *do* have.

The Responsibility Remedy: Examples of What You Can Control

- Where you spend your time and with whom you spend it
- Attitude, work ethic, character choices, discipline, and following processes
- What you eat, whether you exercise, and the overall care you take of your body
- Whether you work to build your mindset each day and throughout the day
- Whether you plan, prepare, or practice
- Whether you learn or grow

- Whether you will seek out feedback, and how you respond to it
- Whether you are coachable, humble, or helpful to others

As you can see, there is much you can control that will make a difference, in contrast to time wasted on what you cannot control or affect.

BIG Bullet: What you give your attention to grows bigger in your life. When it comes to giving attention to what you have no control over, be a miser.

Fred Plays the Victim Card; Frank Calls His Bluff

Frances noticed Fred sitting at his desk, head buried in his hands. "Are you sick, Fred?" she asked.

"Yeah. I'm sick. Sick of this month. My sales are half of what they should be," he replied.

Frances had made this wrong turn and traveled down Blame Boulevard with Fred too often the past eighteen months, so she cut to the chase, "*Why* do you think you're struggling?"

"Where do I start?" he huffed, throwing his hands in the air. "For one thing, no one likes getting out of the house in this weather. Not to mention the economy still hasn't recovered, unemployment is sky high, and our inventory grew stale during the shutdown. Plus, I don't think our advertising is pulling like it did in the past." Fred sharply glanced around the office and leaned in across his desk, saying, "And just between us, I'm not crazy about some of the strategy decisions management has made for moving forward. They seem out of touch in their ivory towers."

Frank, who was passing by and overhead the exchange, chimed in, "I might agree with you, Fred, except for a couple things: My sales are twice what yours are; Frances's are three times higher; and we come to work every day with the same management, advertising, inventory, economy, and weather that you just blamed. Maybe you should look in the mirror and figure out what you can do better. Just saying."

"So, you're 'saying' it's all my fault?" Fred snapped back.

"Pretty much," Frank replied. "And sitting there complaining about it isn't going to make it any better. If I were you, I'd quit whining, get up off my rear end, and do some work. Speaking of which, I'm going to make some calls."

Fred stared bewilderedly at Frances. "Do you think it's okay for him to talk to me that way? He's not my boss."

"He talks to you that way because he likes you, Fred, and he cares about you and wants you to do better. And I agree with him. Get it together and go make something positive happen today. It's still just 10 AM."

Fred, in disbelief, watched Frances as she walked off, then glared over at Frank making calls. He was boiling inside. He wondered how they could gang up on him like this. Every reason he pointed out for his struggles was true. *Just because they're doing better than me doesn't give them the right to be mean*, he thought. *That's the problem with being Mr. Nice Guy—everyone finds it easy to walk all over you*. Fred got up, clocked out for his allotted morning break, and headed for the food truck. A breakfast burrito and a Red Bull always made him feel better.

BIG Bullet: Similar people doing similar things in like conditions with unlike attitudes produce dissimilar results and live unlike lives.

BIG Questions: Is it possible you may focus more on the things you cannot control because it is easier than working on the things you can control? Is doing so a strategy that is going to make it easier or tougher to achieve your *WHY*?

5. I MAINTAIN GRACE UNDER STRESS.

Stress is a given in life. We need certain levels of it to keep us alert and engaged and to help us grow. We all endure stressful moments throughout the day, but how we handle them greatly determines our ABLE and effectiveness. Your current mental state also influences whether stress happens to or for you. Growth and maturity are shown in being able to experience negative or stressful emotions but not reacting to them.

For instance, you can allow stressful situations to make you overreact or panic if you are unfocused, you are void of mental toughness, you have not prepared, and you are not driven by a compelling *WHY* that brings perspective to the provocation at hand. If you are living a comfort-zone lifestyle rather than intentionally building mental toughness by continually raising your basis, stress can quickly blow your state of certainty to smithereens. In contrast, mentally tougher people who have become comfortable being uncomfortable barely break pace when most stressors come calling. They keep their cool, perspective, focus, and ABLE.

In many cases, mentally tougher people consider whatever it is that is creating stress as a challenge or an opportunity to grow and are energized by it. They understand the best time to prepare for stressful situations is before they face them, doing much of what we've discussed in these pages so that they are prepared when the heat comes: intentionally building their mindset daily and setting the table for ABLE; continually changing their basis; and working toward a *WHY* so compelling that it prepares them for, and pulls them through, stressful situations before they can become setbacks.

Being graceful under stress includes the following:

- not overreacting or rushing to judgment with worst-case scenarios
- not shooting the messenger bringing bad news
- not compromising your character to find an easy way out
- avoiding blame, getting personal, and saying or doing something you will have to apologize for later
- refusing to be bullied into making a foolish commitment or compromise to make someone happy or temporarily relieve pressure

- remaining unfazed by the magnitude of a challenge and focusing on the next one right thing you can do now
- taking responsibility and remaining calm
- being kind, courteous, and respectful
- being merciful and treating those who treat you poorly better than they deserve
- maintaining your ABLE while others are unable

BIG Bullet: Mentally tough people do not compromise who they are as a person because of what they feel in a moment.

BIG Question: Are you gracious to those who are peers or under your authority, or primarily only to those whose authority you are under?

6. I AVOID BLAME AND EXCUSES.

Taking responsibility for your actions, your results, and your life can be uncomfortable. It is why people lacking mental toughness are prone to take the pressures of personal responsibility off themselves with excuses or blame. While excuses and blame are character-related, they also result from the wrong attitude. After all, it is an unhealthy mindset that projects everything and everyone else as being the problem or as conspiring to keep one from greater happiness or success.

When Fred has a down month selling, he plays the victim card, saying it was the advertising, his manager, the inventory, or even the customers to fault for his failure.

In the same situation, Frank is prone to admit there are things he could have done better, but still manages to offhandedly weave at least one scapegoat into the conversation: "Of course, the stock market being down is making people hold on to their money and put off large purchases."

Five months ago, when Frances nearly lost her salesperson of the month winning streak to Frank—she won by one sale—she did not shrug it off as a fluke or quip that Frank got all the easy customers. Rather, she admitted she lacked her normally relentless focus and blamed herself for bringing problems with her ex into the workplace and letting it hijack her attention from what mattered most on the job. She created an affirmation she resolved to repeat each time an "ex-thought" trespassed her mindset on the job, and she would shift her mind back into focus by asserting: "Do the most productive thing now."

BIG Bullet: Blame is the anti-focus. Excuses are in the DNA of underachievers. One of the best days of your life is when you subordinate both to the importance of your *WHY*.

BIG Questions: Do you have a "go-to" excuse or scapegoat? If so, how is that working out for you? What goals has it helped you achieve?

7. I MAKE OTHERS FEEL BETTER ABOUT THEMSELVES.

It takes a confident and secure person, and a selfless attitude, to shift one's thinking away from oneself and to build up others. This is especially true when things are not going well for you personally. However, people who do this readily admit that in lifting others they also feel better about themselves.

It is easier to be generous or magnanimous with someone else when everything is going your way. But the true test of character, attitude, and being mentally tough is being able to compliment, encourage, give credit to, or rejoice with another even while your own world may be falling apart. That ability requires graduate-level graciousness, maturity, positivity, and toughness.

It really does not take much to give most people a boost. It can be as simple as:

- giving eye contact and a smile to someone, especially those prone to be ignored or marginalized
- offering a sincere, specific compliment
- actively listening with positive ABLE during a conversation, and letting the other person shine without interrupting, finishing

their sentences for them, or resorting to "been there, done that" one-upmanship

- just listening without trying to fix everything for someone
- quickly forgiving offenses
- doing favors with no expectation of reciprocity
- checking in on someone to see how they are doing and not because you want something
- sharing words of encouragement with someone going through a tough time
- jumping in to help without having to be asked, guilted, threatened, or bribed
- sharing your credit with another
- deflecting praise to someone else
- accepting more than your share of blame
- having empathy for someone making a mistake
- jotting a kind note for a service provider: restaurant worker, flight attendant, hotel housekeeper, and so on
- defending those not present
- tipping more than is customary
- sticking up for someone despite being outnumbered
- choosing to remain silent rather than projecting a critical spirit that nitpicks things that do not really matter
- expressing gratitude

BIG Bullet: "It is one of the beautiful compensations in this life that no one can sincerely try to help another without helping himself."[21] —Ralph Waldo Emerson

BIG Question: Throughout the day, do you make an intentional effort to make people feel better about themselves?

YOU NEED POSITIVITY *AND* OPTIMISM

Mentally tough people who control their attitude blend positivity with optimism. These are two different and essential traits. Being positive is about today: thinking productively, employing constructive words and actions, having an approach with others that builds them up, and maintaining a focus on what is useful regardless of what is going on around you.

Optimism concerns a confidence in the future. Some people are very positive today but dread what is coming next: "Let's make the most out of today, guys, because who knows if we'll be in business next month." Others can find little good in a current situation, day, or week, but believe down the road things will get better: "Today really stinks, but tomorrow's a better day!" An intentional mindset is built by avoiding the "either/or" aspect of these two traits and instead delivering positivity *and* optimism. It is about being both. In fact, positivity and optimism are so closely joined that being constructive, productive, and useful today gives you the right to be legitimately optimistic about the future. On the other hand, those who are not constructive, productive, or useful today in their thinking or actions have no business feeling optimistic about a better future. Why should they when they are not doing what is necessary now to create it? At best, they are wishful thinkers.

BIG Bullet: Legitimate optimism for tomorrow is earned by how you think and what you do today.

The benefits of intentionally building your mindset by intensely working on your attitude for a week during the ACCREDITED course are nearly limitless. As you work on these seven aspects you will influence your mental toughness and killer instinct meaningfully and consistently, and your ABLE will show it!

INTENTIONAL ACTION

Review these seven aspects each morning during your mindset routine for the next week to heighten your awareness for improvement opportunities throughout the day.

BADGERS ADVERSITY INCIDENT #5

November 25–December 11, 2019: Badgers Lose Four out of Five Games

Despite their slow start and disappointing news concerning Micah Potter, the Badgers redoubled their efforts to get on track and find a rhythm.

During this difficult stretch, the Badgers struggled to find their identity as a team. They would stay in contention for the duration of the games, only to let the contests slip away in the waning minutes. The Badgers had lost their star senior player, Ethan Happ, from the year before and looked lost at times. Who would step up? What were they missing? How could they toughen up and close out games to finish what they started? Without answers to these questions, the team found itself in a rut. After the loss to Rutgers on December 11, Coach Gard challenged the men's toughness and tenacity—major assets the team had built a reputation on and had become known for but that seemed missing at the time.

PLAY A POOR HAND WELL

- What is your first step for working yourself out of a rut?
- Are you aware of what puts you in ruts in the first place?
- Are you prone to start things well but not to finish? What can you do to create more compelling reasons for finishing?
- In which areas of your life do you lack mental toughness and how can you change that?

Chapter Six

COMPETITIVENESS

Go from Common Participant to Commonly Dominant

Consider the definition of *compete*: "strive to gain or win something by defeating or establishing superiority over others who are trying to do the same."[22]

Within the context of *Intentional Mindset,* "competitiveness" is about competing with our former selves in a lifelong daily challenge for self-improvement in the ACCREDITED traits, consistently raising our levels of mental toughness and killer instinct so that we are equipped to achieve even the most compelling aspects of our *WHY.* Thus, we will repurpose the definition of "compete" in the following context:

To strive to gain or win something: The objective is to win victory over our former self (who we were yesterday, last week, six months ago, sixty years ago) by purposefully improving the ACCREDITED traits essential for building mental toughness and a killer instinct.

By defeating or establishing superiority over others who are trying to do the same: We want to compete with ourselves (more than others) and be superior in the seven aspects of competitiveness we will cover in this chapter: attitude, habits, focus, discipline, knowledge, drive, energy, motivation, and results. Waging this war of improvement against our

> former selves is essential to combating complacency and creating the healthy discomfort we need to become all we are intended to be as human beings, and to accomplish all we are endowed to achieve.

For competitive people, the idea of competing with one's self more than with others can seem unnatural. After all, winning is normally considered as something you do over another person or organization. But coming out on top of someone else is a hollow victory if you are not personally improving; you beat them simply because they were worse than you. Sure, it is still a "win." But the reality is you can win in that manner and still be in decline, become complacent and deluded about your abilities as a result, and never address the decline because you are unaware it is happening. We cannot control how well another person prepares, how they will use their talent, how hard they will work, or how well they will execute; this is why competing with our former selves is empowering. We can control the effort and outcome.

When you compete primarily with yourself, you continually raise your standards so that even if you fall short of your personal expectations, you blow away what others expected of you.

BIG Bullet: "When you reach for the stars you may not quite get one, but you won't come up with a handful of mud either."[23] —Leo Burnett

SEVEN KEY ASPECTS OF COMPETITIVENESS

1. MY ATTITUDE IS SUPERIOR TO YESTERDAY'S.

In case you missed my nudge in the previous chapter, let me not so subtly reiterate: When you see a recurring theme (as is the case here with attitude) appearing in multiple places throughout the book, it is worth taking notice, because the additional emphasis highlights its importance to building mental toughness and a killer instinct.

The goal here is to handle aspects like the seven on attitude listed in the previous chapter better with each new day than you did the day before. Let's quickly refresh on the aspects of attitude:

- Responding well to negative things
- Not being easily offended
- Demonstrating positive speech
- Focusing on what you can control
- Maintaining grace under stress
- Avoiding blame and excuses
- Using words and actions to make others feel better about themselves

Using the Personal Progress Diary when you complete this book to evaluate and grade yourself on living all seven aspects of a particular ACCREDITED trait at day's end as part of the follow-up course will help create greater awareness of where you must compete harder with your past performance to improve. For instance, if on Monday, when grading yourself on the attitude aspect of competitiveness, you realize that you made an excuse for being late to a meeting rather than admit you wrote the wrong time down, you can correct your course on Tuesday and beat Monday's score by having a heightened awareness of excuses and more resolve to take responsibility for your actions.

BIG Bullet: Your attitude is never a secret you can keep for long.

BIG Questions: What attitude letdown did you demonstrate yesterday? Are you intentional about improving that aspect today?

2. MY HABITS ARE SUPERIOR TO YESTERDAY'S.

Habits are behaviors that we repeat so often that they are automatic. We do them without thinking. Depending on what they are, your habits can work for or against you. Building an intentional mindset is about developing both the discipline to do more of the right things and the self-control to avoid what is unproductive—executing both so well and for so long that we build right habits and eliminate wrong ones.

We will dig more deeply into discipline and habits in chapter ten, but for now, know that competing with yesterday's habits can include strengthening your exercise or eating habits, improving your mindset or personal growth routines, productively using drive time while commuting or downtime at home, and more. And as you will find with many aspects of this and the other ACCREDITED traits, progress can also come from areas where you are trying to lower your basis. In terms of habits this could include wasting less time at work, watching less television, swearing less frequently, or drinking less alcohol.

BIG Bullet: Habits are cultivated, not commanded.

BIG Questions: Which unproductive or undeveloped habit has held you back for too long? What is your plan today to intentionally improve that habit?

3. MY FOCUS IS SUPERIOR TO YESTERDAY'S.

Whatever we focus on in our lives gets bigger: problems or solutions; things we can or cannot control; people who elevate us or devastate us; activities that inspire us or just tire us; and more. It is up to us to choose well, which is why it is so vital that we consistently work to give attention to the activities and people that matter most. They are what makes it easier rather than more difficult to achieve our *WHY*. This reaffirms why the sharper focus gained by intentionally working on your mindset in the morning before the action starts is essential to maximizing the moments and opportunities within each day.

BIG Bullet: The question is not whether you have focus, because everyone focuses on something. The point is recognizing the impact of what you are focusing on has in achieving your goals each day.

BIG Questions: What most often interrupts your focus on what is productive? How can you minimize or remove that influence from your day?

4. MY DISCIPLINE IS SUPERIOR TO YESTERDAY'S.

Discipline fuels habits. Thus, the stronger your progress on discipline, the more your habits grow stronger. Impossible without self-control, discipline subordinates temporary feelings to a better future. The strength of your *WHY* will significantly impact your discipline because once you have locked in on what matters most in life, it is easier to have the control to say "No" to the things and people making it tougher to get them. But until you have narrowed your focus on a bold and compelling *WHY*, you are prone to drift, go through the motions, mistake motion for progress, confuse activity with accomplishment, and mistake speed for direction.

Prioritize Your Future over Your Feelings

Alex was the type of sales manager who always started meetings on time, so at 8 AM sharp, the team was fully assembled in the training room and ready to go.

Alex kicked things off with a question. "What is our minimum required standard of sales calls daily?"

Fred, thinking this might be the only opportunity he would get a question right during the next hour, seized the chance and rightly proclaimed, "Ten!"

Alex smiled, "So you do know the number, Fred? The reason I ask is that you rarely, if ever, manage to make all ten calls. Why is that?"

Fred stared back. Stupefied and shocked to be called out in front of the group, he immediately regretted his decision to speak up.

Alex grilled on: "Is it because you don't *feel* like making the calls on some days? Or maybe you *feel* like you're wasting time calling some customers back because you've determined they're not going to buy? Or maybe the time you spent with them didn't *feel* enjoyable because they were tough, unfriendly, or appeared unqualified, and deep down you didn't *feel* like seeing them again?"

Fred sat frozen. Every reason that Alex mentioned was true. *Is Alex reading my mind?* he thought. Fred needed a burrito and a Red Bull in the worst way right now. As Alex turned his attention to Frank, Fred let out a huge sigh of relief and thought to himself, *Man, that is the last time I will ever do* that *again*.

"How many calls do you make every day, Frank?" Alex questioned.

"I never miss my ten calls, boss."

"Are there days you could do more?"

Frank jabbed back, "I guess so, but the objective is ten, right?"

"Ten is the minimum number we require. It's baseline. If you have extra time, would it help your sales to make more calls?"

Frank was miffed. "Hang on, let me get this straight. So, you're gonna call me out for doing my job, Alex? Ten is my job." Nodding toward Fred, Frank continued, "Apparently, it's better than some guys are doing. And by the way, Alex, how can management even call ten the standard if when guys don't do it, there's no consequence? Because that's what is happening now with a few guys in this room."

Fred, meanwhile having worked his way toward the back of the training room for a second bagel, stifled a chuckle and looked around trying to make eye contact with anyone he could talk with later about the drama that was now unfolding in front of them—perhaps when the breakfast truck rolled around. Now it was Alex's turn to squirm because Frank was right. There was no consequence for not making the ten calls. In Fred's case, he liked the guy and wanted him to make it with the company, so he went easy on him. In retrospect, maybe that had not been the best strategy since Fred's performance never improved. Evading Frank's question, Alex shifted the group's attention to Frances, "How many calls you do you make each day, Frances?"

"All I can. Some days it's fifteen, others it's twenty, occasionally it's more. I always try to beat the number I made the day before."

"Why bother, Frances? Frank doesn't," Alex replied.

"To me, ten is the company's standard, and that's fine, but I have a higher standard for myself than you could ever have for me, and that's to push hard and do all I can."

Alex pressed, "What do you do on the days you don't feel like making the calls?"

"There are plenty of days I don't feel like making calls, but I know the calls work. They're what leads to sales, so on those days I have to decide what's more important: my feelings or my future. I guess the bottom line is that regardless of how I feel, why would I do less than I'm capable of doing? That just makes no sense to me. To do less than I can seems like stealing from myself, my family, my teammates, my future, and the company."

The other nine salespeople in the room looked straight ahead. Their conscience and conduct had been convicted and called out. Alex was ecstatic. Frances made a stronger point to them as their peer than he could ever make as their manager. Frances had ended the meeting with a mic drop and, not wanting to screw it up, Alex closed the meeting, saying, "This meeting's a wrap. Let's go make some calls."

BIG Bullet: Some will do some, some won't do many, and some don't stop doing what some won't do at all.

Act your way into feeling; don't feel your way into acting. If you live life *feeling* your way into acting, you will jeopardize your future by failing to take action simply because you don't *feel* like it. If you subordinate your feelings to your future and *act* your way into feeling even when you would rather do nothing, you will *feel* better afterward because you did something to help your future.

BIG Bullet: Discipline is giving up what you want now for what you want most.

BIG Questions: What productive activity did you not feel like doing today that you did anyway? Did you feel better about yourself when you were finished?

5. MY KNOWLEDGE IS SUPERIOR TO YESTERDAY'S.

Growth is not automatic. You must seek out and apply new knowledge because life is not likely to come along, interrupt you, and improve you.

If you are listening to podcasts, reading the right books, taking online courses, applying lessons from your experiences, seeking out feedback, picking the brains of wise friends and peers, and more, you are far more likely to enlarge your knowledge base and make yourself more valuable so you can add more value and achieve the valuables you have outlined in your *WHY*.

BIG Bullet: Intellectual capital depreciates. Wisdom is knowing what you must learn, as well as what you must unlearn.

BIG Questions: Have you gotten lazy in your learning? What is the one next productive thing you can do today to change that?

6. MY DRIVE/ENERGY/MOTIVATION IS SUPERIOR TO YESTERDAY'S.

Oftentimes your *WHY* is compelling enough to force you to bring more drive, energy, and motivation every day, but you are still not doing it because you have lost touch with that *WHY*. As the saying goes: out of sight, out of mind. The world has distracted you from it with worries and concerns you cannot control, or perhaps it has lost its relevance and you need to revisit and redefine it so that you can get refocused on it.

When your *WHY* is clear and compelling enough, you will not need external motivators to get you going because you will already be in gear. Any affirmation you get from others is always nice, but it is just not as necessary because you are on fire from within and do not require your flames to be fanned from the outside in.

Sometimes it can feel as though your drive, energy, or motivation have plateaued. While plateauing at a high level is not all bad, there is still certainly room to compete with yesterday's levels and improve. It might be taking in less media, getting higher-quality sleep, eating better, exercising more, consuming less alcohol, or engaging with fewer people and activities that dampen drive or drain energy that can help you take it up a notch.

BIG Bullet: Provoke and channel drive. Clarify and embolden motivators. Feed and manage energy.

BIG Questions: Do you have a harder time starting fast or finishing well? What will you do to improve both aspects?

7. MY RESULTS ARE SUPERIOR TO YESTERDAY'S.

While it is natural to measure the success of a day, week, month, game, or contest by its outcome, there is more to measuring results than tallying scores. Since executing the right activities is most predictive of achieving a desired result, those must also be factored into evaluating one's results at day's end. This may change how you judge a day. For instance, there are days when many things you have been working on for the past few weeks all come together to create an outstanding result, despite the fact you may have done little that is productive on that particular day. Would you necessarily evaluate your performance that day as being outstanding? Perhaps not.

On the other hand, there are many other days when you may execute high-impact activities with excellence and consistency during the day but have little to show for it, at least on that particular day. Would you write that day off as a failure? Of course not.

Thus, when you are grading yourself on the results you are responsible for attaining in your line of work, as a team member, a student, and so on, you should weigh both the execution of high-impact activities most predictive of creating desired outcomes and the outcomes themselves. The ultimate day would be one that sees fruit borne from past efforts, in addition to good seeds planted for future results. The worst possible scenario would be seeing no tangible outcomes from past efforts, while at the same time being unable or unwilling to engage in the high-impact activities that would change that picture in the future.

BIG Bullet: In life, as in farming, not every season is a harvest. There are seasons of planting, weeding, watering, spraying, and seeding that create the harvest. But it is foolish and futile to go to the ground and demand a crop where no sowing had been done.

BIG Question: Do you make an intentional effort to balance the art of creating a result today, while also planting seeds for a future result tomorrow?

EVERY DAY A NEW ADVENTURE

When you build an intentional mindset in which your primary challenge each day is to be better in critically important areas than you were the day before, every day is more exciting, meaningful, challenging, and energizing. Day after day is like a game in which you compete with the scores you created yesterday.

You know you are not always going to win, but the thrill of battle and the chance to do it better today than yesterday is exhilarating. With an intentional mindset you no longer approach a day to get through it but to gain from it, building the mental toughness and killer instinct you need to convert your most compelling *WHY* into a thrilling and fulfilling reality.

INTENTIONAL ACTION

Review your written *WHY* and honestly answer these questions:

- Is it really compelling enough to make me want to compete with myself and improve in these areas daily?
- Is it really compelling enough to leave me no option but to subordinate my feelings and take action to build a better future?
- Is it really compelling enough to make me hunger for a life in which I become comfortable being uncomfortable because I know that only as I become more can I get more, impact more, and achieve more?

If you are the least bit unsure that any of these answers would be a resounding *yes*, then you must take the time to reevaluate your life and become clearer and bolder concerning who you want to become, what you would like to get and achieve, who you would like to help or impact, and what legacy you want to leave.

BADGERS ADVERSITY INCIDENT #6

January 8, 2020: Badgers Blow Late Lead in Rare Home Loss to Illinois 71–70

After losing four of five games through mid-December, the Badgers looked forward to hosting conference rival Illinois for a home game in early January.

After leading by seven points with time winding down, the Badgers again lost control of the game and could not finish an opponent, even on their home court. After making progress the past few games, they regressed and reverted to their old ways from earlier in the season.

PLAY A POOR HAND WELL

- What mistakes during your life have you been most prone to repeat, whether morally based, skills-based, relationship-based, attitude-based, or something else? How can you stop reverting to those unhealthy mindsets or behaviors?
- How do you respond when you lose in an area in which you were expected to win? How can you make your response more productive and lessen the chances you will lose in the same manner again?
- In which routines do you lack the most consistency: mindset, health and exercise, work-related, spiritual, relationships, or something else? What is a strategy you can use to improve consistency in those areas?

Chapter Seven

CHARACTER

Cultivate a Rock-Solid Moral Code

Character can be defined as the moral and/or ethical traits that make up the individual nature of a person. Character is influenced by many things throughout our lives, but especially by our values and belief systems. It is either cultivated or diminished during the course of our lives as we make decisions based on those values and beliefs, embrace or amend values and beliefs, and ignore or discard the values and beliefs we once had.

BIG Bullet: Strong character protects and helps leverage assets like talent, skills, knowledge, and experience. It ensures the assets you have are applied rightly, with correct motives, even when life gets difficult or things do not go your way.

CHARACTER AT THE ROOT

Fred does not take responsibility for his results and is prone to blame conditions and others when he falls short. This is a character issue.

Frank is tardy on occasion and is also prone to dismiss valid feedback intended to improve his performance because his better-than-average success has made him mostly unteachable. These are matters of character that he can change but that no one else can change for him.

Frances routinely does more than is required and often offers to help teammates who are struggling. Frances was not born this way. She became this way by choosing personal standards and values that do not allow otherwise. These character strengths are strongly responsible for the consistency of her results, including her fifteen-month winning streak atop the sales board.

BIG Bullet: You can try to influence another person's character choices, but you cannot change it or them. You can change yourself, and you can do so immediately; so, start there.

IT'S NO GUARANTEE

As important as it is to have a clear and compelling *WHY,* it is no guarantee you will make the right character choices. In fact, you can go astray craving your *WHY* so intensely that you engage in unproductive or unethical behaviors to achieve it, rationalizing that the end justifies your means.

Your character has been forming since you were old enough to reason intelligently, and by building an intentional mindset you can productively cultivate it and make its continual improvement your life's work. To maintain a hunger and diligence to improve your character, it is important to grasp that character is never "finished" but is forever strengthened or diminished based on how you think and act. Thus, to improve your character you must be more intentional.

As with all the ACCREDITED traits, the seven aspects listed for character are not all that matter in its development but are highly influential to building a mindset that not only fuels your killer instinct and mental toughness, but helps you sustain your success over time by helping you avoid unproductive decisions and behaviors that would cause you to self-destruct.

To reinforce a similar point I shared in chapter five, the seven specific aspects of character you will work to improve and grade yourself on daily during the follow-up ACCREDITED course are to be done within the context of how you performed character-wise in all of life's arenas: filing your income taxes; keeping commitments to your spouse, children, and teammates; admitting fault for a misunderstanding; dealing financially with clients; applying for a loan; taking an exam; and more.

SEVEN KEY ASPECTS OF CHARACTER

1. I AM HONEST IN WORDS AND DEEDS.

It is common to believe that honesty is solely about being truthful, but that is just half the equation. Honesty also encompasses freedom from deceit. A habitual occurrence for those whose conscience will not let them lie outright is to tell a half-truth, create a false impression, or withhold the truth altogether. While what they have done cannot be classified as a flat-out "lie," it is nonetheless designed to make someone believe something that is not true. In cases like this, the conscience you tried to protect by not telling an official lie is pricked nonetheless, as you know within your soul you were dishonest.

The Power of Affirmations

As part of Frances's morning mindset routine, she reads a list of affirmations she has created for herself that defines how she wants to think, act, and become as a person. These affirmations help create a standard she holds herself to each day. Affirmations strengthen the wiring in her mind each morning so that right thinking and behaviors become more automatic—part of her essence. One affirmation that has helped her build a loyal following of customers who trust her completely is, "I say what's true and do what's right *every time*." As simple as that single sentence is, it establishes a powerful accountability benchmark that she aspires to reach daily.

 **BIG Bullet:** A guilty conscience is a mindset massacre.

 **BIG Questions:** Where are you prone to not lie outright but to create a false impression instead? Do you realize that people tend to secretly despise those they discover are deceptive?

2. I ACCEPT RESPONSIBILITY.

In an age of blame, where "It's not my fault" has become the mantra of many, taking responsibility for your decisions, actions, results, and life delivers key benefits, five of which are:

- It allows you to learn and improve from mistakes.
- It builds trust and draws people to you as others rally around the humility and coachability of those who own it.
- It keeps your focus and energy directed at the things you can control, rather than wasting them on scapegoats.
- It earns respect and reputation.
- In doing so, you build both self-esteem and self-respect.

While obvious, it is also worth mentioning that failing to accept responsibility does the opposite:

- You fail to grow, and you repeat the same errors.
- It stops others from investing in you, wanting to help you, and giving you new opportunities.
- It causes you to engage in one of the lowest-return endeavors of human behavior: investing focus and energy into things you cannot control.
- It causes others to disrespect you and harms your reputation.
- You naturally feel worse about yourself when suffering the four points described above.

Incidentally, taking responsibility is not just about the big things; once you rationalize enough "little" things, the next bigger deviation is easier to excuse. This includes 'fessing up to the mess, eating the last cookie, admitting what you actually said, and not blaming the dog when that toxic torpedo escapes your intestines after chowing on chili.

BIG Bullet: "If you could kick the person in the pants responsible for most of your trouble, you wouldn't sit for a month."[24] —Theodore Roosevelt

BIG Questions: What do you have the hardest time owning up to? Can you sense the freedom in being able to say, "This is on me"?

3. I KEEP MY COMMITMENTS.

This one is often a no-brainer when it is easy, cheap, popular, or convenient to keep the commitment. But strong character is about doing what you said you would when it is not those things. Consider these four points on commitments.

- Be careful which commitments you make because once you make it, you are expected to keep it without excuse and regardless of the cost.
- Do not let someone pressure you into making a commitment. Do not promise something you will later regret just to make them happy. That is just another form of instant gratification that weaker-minded people fall for as a means of relieving momentary discomfort.
- If for some reason you are unable to keep a commitment, own it and make it up to whomever you let down.
- If reading this causes you to recall unkept commitments in the past, reconcile quickly with that person. I can promise you the offended party has not forgotten, and they do not understand your failure, despite the fact you likely convinced yourself they have and they do. In fact, failing to address your unkept commitment is likely creating

bitterness that will stew within someone, causing them to eventually overreact to something you say or do, and in some cases to seek vengeance.

BIG Bullet: "Unexpressed emotions will never die. They are buried alive and will come forth later in uglier ways."[25] —Sigmund Freud

Tardiness Is a Heart Issue

If someone on a team is likely to be tardy, most teammates can pretty well predict who it will be. They are repeat offenders, dismissing tardiness with "I was busy," "Traffic was bad," "It's only five minutes," or "I've got to get better organized." But it is not that simple. Tardiness is not a head issue where you habitually forget to leave on time so that you can arrive on time. It is a heart issue, a matter of character. Why? Because when you are late you are failing to keep a commitment you made to someone else, and that reflects on your character.

Tardiness is also considered a character flaw because it shows disrespect for others: You are not at work to do your part, so others may become overwhelmed and have to pick up your slack; you abuse others' irreplaceable time as they wait on you to arrive for meetings or events; and more.

To make a point, I tell attendees at my seminars that if they are going to steal from me, I prefer they take my money and leave my time alone, because I can get more money but I cannot get more time. Having rock-solid character is not just about having a high regard for your own time, but for the time of others as well.

BIG Bullet: If others continually discover they cannot count on you, they are prone to reconsider whether they need you at all.

BIG Questions: In which areas do you need to become less rash in making a commitment you will regret later? To whom have you failed to keep a commitment that you need to make right?

4. I GIVE COMPLETE EFFORT AT WORK.

If Fred and Frank were to honestly rank themselves on this aspect of character, they would fall short most days. The exceptions are the instances when time in the month is running out, and they are behind in the company's goal for them to such an extent that there could be complete embarrassment or accountability repercussions; or, when they are lagging in the personal income goal they set for the month and need an extra push to make enough money for their bills.

Neither man looks at his lack of complete effort each day as a character flaw that is robbing his employer, his family, and his future. They instead dismiss it as unimportant based on the number of people in their workplace that do so similarly.

With an intentionally built mindset powered by a compelling *WHY*, you cannot afford to let yourself slack at your role, whether it is in the workplace, caring for a household, raking the yard, playing on a team, cleaning your room, or more. You won't let yourself slack because the stakes are too high, the reasons for *not* giving less than you can are too clear, and your time on this Earth is too short.

BIG Bullet: Doing less than you can eventually makes you less than you are.

BIG Questions: In which aspect(s) of your life must you become more intentional about giving your complete effort? Have you ever considered that holding back effort from someone who is counting on you is a subtle form of stealing from them?

5. I PUT OTHERS FIRST.

As discussed in the prior points, if you do not keep commitments or arrive on time, you are flunking the aspect of character that puts others first. Putting others' welfare above your own demonstrates a serving spirit that builds your own self-esteem and confidence. While reciprocity should not be your driving motive, putting others first demonstrates a belief in it: As you help others and serve them, those right and kindhearted acts will also return in kind to lift you in times of need. Putting others first involves seemingly small actions that reflect selflessness, such as:

- listening to others with the intent to understand them
- troubling yourself on someone else's behalf by investing time or effort in assisting them
- encouraging or complimenting others, even when you feel down
- sharing knowledge, experience, or wisdom with those less informed
- giving away or deflecting credit or praise to others
- letting others go first
- letting hungry Uncle Ralph have the last drumstick
- holding the door open for others
- opening the car door for your significant other
- letting someone else pick the movie
- being the last in your group to go through the buffet line
- turning off the lights and putting trash in the cans before checking out of a hotel room

A healthy and intentional mindset is heavily focused on serving versus being served. In fact, as you may have discovered when going through the *WHY* workbook, two of the categories (external and legacy) are completely about impacting others, while developing the personal traits you aspire to improve in the virtue category will strongly influence your effect on others as well.

BIG Bullet: "People who live for themselves are in a mighty small business."[26] —John Maxwell

BIG Questions: In which area(s) of your life have you become unconsciously selfish? Do you believe that those who want to be truly great must first serve others?

6. I CONTROL MY TONGUE.

This is an umbrella aspect, covering everything that comes out of your mouth or through your written words. The fact this aspect overlaps with many other actions found within the ACCREDITED traits highlights how important it is and why it is essential to become more intentional in this regard. Here are some pointers to consider:

- Growth in wisdom is knowing what to overlook and what does not matter enough to weigh in on.
- You do not always need to have the last word.
- You do not have to accept an invitation to every argument or debate.
- You do not have to correct everyone and put them in their place.
- It is not necessary to issue commentary or judgment on everyone and everything you observe.
- Sometimes something needs to be said, but not now; timing is important.
- When it comes to speaking intelligently, less is more. The longer you ramble on, the more you increase the odds you will say something unproductive, regrettable, or outright stupid.
- *How* you say what you say often carries more weight than what you say because it reflects attitude and motives—the true state of your heart.
- Written words like texts, emails, or what you post on social media count as your spoken words.
- If you do not know what to say, say nothing.
- If what you say will not add value, say nothing.
- Speed—being too fast to complain, gossip, criticize, judge, debate, and respond—is often the enemy of healthy speech.
- Instant replies to provocations or bad news often avail nothing but strife.

If most people were to evaluate at day's end every word they said over the course of it, they would likely conclude that a very small percentage of it actually added value, solved anything, made the world a better place, or was necessary at all. Misspent words misuse energy and divert focus away from a *WHY* that matters most and onto a *what* that often means little or nothing.

BIG Bullet: Your "two cents' worth" can cost you a fortune. If in doubt, leave it out.

BIG Questions: What is your biggest challenge in this regard: what you say, how you say it, or when you say it? What will help you become a more intentional controller of the tongue?

7. I REMAIN HUMBLE AND TEACHABLE.

If you brag about being humble, you're not. And, there is no way you will put in the time and effort to develop an intentional mindset if you are not humble or teachable, primarily because you will not see the need for improvement in areas you should and could improve. Sure, you may give it a shot for a while, but sooner or later, the "What's all the fuss about?" mental conversation will hijack your once-good intentions, especially if you have become more successful along the way and do not see the need to further change anything. This is a prideful state of mind, and pride (an overinflated value of oneself) eventually becomes arrogance (believing you are superior to others).

Combating pride and arrogance with humility and teachability is precisely why working on the competitiveness trait discussed in the previous chapter is so important: It shifts your focus away from measuring yourself against others and causes you to compete primarily with yourself.

While pride comes naturally, humility must be cultivated. You must intentionally work at it. Your humility is what opens the way for teachability, while pride is what bars the door shut.

Below are key points to consider when evaluating your humility and teachability.

- How do you respond to constructive feedback? Are you more interested in being "right" than in getting better?

- How do you respond to critics? Do you dismiss them offhandedly or consider that even an inkling of what they say might be useful?
- How do you handle unfair situations? Is your first response to get even, or to get better?
- How do you handle success? Does it turn you into a know-it-all, or make you hungry for more? Does prosperity influence you to let up or to use your momentum to step up further?
- When things do not go your way, are you focused more on how you deserve better, or on learning to handle it better?
- Do you crave or deflect praise?
- Are you into serving, or being served?
- Do you push yourself to the front or trust that your character and/or performance will cause you to eventually rise to the front?
- Do you make conversations about yourself or put your focus on others?
- Can you listen to others without diminishing what they say or trying to top it?
- Are you genuinely happy for the success of others?
- Does a rival's success make you want to get better or bitter? Do you secretly wish them ill?
- When you are right, and you know you are right, can you still express yourself humbly?
- Do your biases or prejudices cause you to feel superior to someone different than you? Do you look down on, or talk down to, those considered in lower stations of life due to age, position, power, or possessions?
- Are you respectful and kind to those who are subordinate to you in status within your organization?
- Do you consider training, reading an assigned book, taking an assigned course, or attending a seminar as an opportunity or as a punishment?

We could go on with examples for many pages, but these points cover good and ample ground. And here is a clue: If you thought primarily about how someone else was failing miserably in any of the points listed, then you missed the point entirely!

BIG Bullet: If you are not sure where you are prideful and need to become humbler and more teachable, ask those who know you best; they have known for quite some time.

BIG Questions: Did any of the sixteen bullet points listed make you uncomfortable? Circle them. Can you replay the most recent instance concerning that aspect in your mind and determine up front how you will handle something similar in a more productive manner next time?

CHARACTER: YOUR LEVER AND SHIELD

Character leverages your skills, knowledge, talent, and experience by helping you stay out of your own way so you can maximize those assets. It also protects them from self-destructive tendencies because strong character protects you from taking shortcuts; making unhealthy compromises; disregarding others; and becoming intellectually irrelevant, socially undesirable, or selfish. It shields you from temptations like instant gratification, blame, excuses, and dishonesty.

Speaking of blame and excuses, the fact you may have had poor influences in your life in regard to character, or that you have them now, does not give you permission to do likewise. They may have had, or are having now, a detrimental effect on you, but as chapter four pointed out: It is your decisions more than conditions that ultimately determine how far you go and how fast you get there. And you must own those decisions.

BIG Bullet: It is not enough to know better. To grow, you must do better.

INTENTIONAL ACTION

Create a one-sentence affirmation that describes the productive counterpart to each character flaw you recognized within yourself and review it as part of your intentional mindset routine each morning. For instance, if you are weak in keeping commitments you might say, "I consider the cost before I commit, then pay the price to deliver what I commit."

BADGERS ADVERSITY INCIDENT #7

January 17, 2020: Badgers Outperformed in Embarrassing Loss to Michigan State 67–55

The Badgers had a chance to create major momentum in January, especially after their wins against two top-twenty-five teams in a row. A win against conference rival Michigan State would shift that momentum into overdrive.

After consecutively beating two top-twenty-five teams, Penn State and Maryland, the Badgers again failed to leverage their momentum and continue their run. Despite desperately wanting a third consecutive top-tier victory to establish a rhythm and build a confidence they would need for the final eight weeks of the season, they were outplayed by their opponent from start to finish.

PLAY A POOR HAND WELL

- How can you stay motivated when you are making progress and getting on a roll toward your goals, only to take a major step back?
- When you get knocked down after doing well, do you make matters worse by staying down too long because of fear, discouragement, exhaustion, or lack of inspiration? How can you decide up front to make a better choice the next time something like that happens? Is there an affirmation you can create that would keep your mindset focused in those instances?

Chapter Eight

RIGOR

Design a Relentless Daily Regimen

Rigor is "the quality of being extremely thorough, exhaustive, or accurate."[27] In the context of this chapter and throughout the follow-up ACCREDITED course, rigor applies to having a highly structured daily routine that allows you to get more of the right things done, both consistently and with excellence. In other words, you will work more intensely on the things that matter most and continue to find better ways to do those things as you compete with your former self and improve.

An intentional mindset helps you purposefully identify and execute your priorities on a given day and consciously work to improve your ability to perform them. Everyone has a daily routine; that is not the question. The questions are:

- What is your daily routine helping you to become?
- Is your daily routine taking you to your *WHY* or making it tougher to get there?
- How often do you reevaluate, tweak, and look to improve your daily routine so that you can accelerate progress and growth?

BIG Bullet: "I have learned that champions aren't just born; champions can be made when they embrace and commit to life-changing, positive habits."[28]
—Lewis Howes

ALL ROUTINES MATTER

Routines are effective, which is why their existence is so widespread amongst all of life's spheres, including:

- work
- personal growth
- fitness
- relationships
- downtime
- time at home with family
- spirituality
- finances (budgeting and saving)

The goal of rigor is to develop better routines in all these key areas of life, which can be done by taking the principles in this chapter and adapting them to enhance your routines.

BIG Bullet: Human beings develop to their potential in structured environments. The goal is to get *from* a day, not just through it.

A HIGH REGARD FOR TIME

Time is more than just money. Truly it is more valuable than money, because while you can get more money, you cannot get more time than what you already have. Without an intentional mindset, it is highly unlikely you will have a high regard for time or rigor in your day because you will not know which tasks to start attacking each day—what you must say yes or no to throughout the day. And without an intentional mindset, you can be sure once getting off track during the day you are likely to stay there. Rigor compresses focus and energy into what matters most, every day. It fosters discipline and enables consistency. But until you have a regard for time that goes beyond clichés like "Life is short" and "Make the most of each day," you will spend your days a mile wide and an inch deep, leaving a blur rather than a mark in your wake. You must respect time, value it, and appreciate that it is finite—and therefore avoid tasks, thoughts, and people that waste it. And make no mistake, people with nothing to do will want to do it with you!

Following are seven daily focus points for rigor that you will evaluate and learn from during the follow-up ACCREDITED course.

SEVEN KEY ASPECTS OF RIGOR

1. I SCHEDULE MY PRIORITIES IN ADVANCE.

The sage advice to "prioritize your schedule" will not help you if you are prioritizing the wrong things. Fred's priority is being first in line for the food truck each morning as it rounds the corner at 10 AM, but that is not helping him grow unless you count his girth. Peter Drucker put prioritizing into perspective with his succinct guidance, "First things first, and second things not at all."[29] The problem for many people is wrongly classifying easy things, hard things, or last things left over from yesterday's to-do list as first things. In doing so, they engage in activities that cause them to not spend much if any time at all on the true "first things" —the highest-impact activities most predictive of taking them to their *WHY* each day.

A key to daily rigor in your routine is to stop trying to squeeze your priorities into the day, but instead to schedule your priorities and work the day around them.

BIG Bullet: Priorities are not necessarily the good or great things, but the best things. Too often, it is the good and great that edge out the best.

BIG Questions: Do you know what your work priorities are before you leave for work? Are they scheduled on your calendar or scattered in your mind?

2. I SUCCESSFULLY EXECUTE MY PRIORITIES.

While scheduling priorities is a necessary and vital starting place for daily rigor, doing so does not guarantee you will do them, do them with excellence, or do them with consistency. Echoing a theme discussed in chapter six concerning competitiveness, the goal is not only to do the highest-impact activities but to continue to find ways to do them better by competing with your former self.

BIG Bullet: Effective execution is not about getting a lot done, but getting the best things done with excellence, every day.

BIG Question: Are you more inclined to measure a day by how much you got done, or by whether the most essential things were done?

3. MY DAILY ROUTINE IS MORE EFFECTIVE THAN YESTERDAY'S.

You can schedule and execute your daily priorities with excellence and still not maximize your daily routine at work if you are off track in life's other vital areas. Did your morning begin with a mindset routine that channels your killer instinct and reinforces mental toughness? Were you fully engaged with family and friends, or merely physically present while being mentally detached as you pondered who to start at quarterback on your fantasy football team? In addition to focusing on your priorities, did you consciously avoid the conversations, people, habits, and distractions that made executing them well impossible?

Live in Tomorrow Versus Maximize Today

When Fred does not have a productive day, he rationalizes it, saying, "I can make it up tomorrow" or "There's plenty of time left in the month," thereby draining his drive and excusing his inability to perform. This "throw-away day" rationalization is common with underachievers, causing them to spend much of their life living in the land of "someday." The problem with residing there is it takes all pressure off performing well today.

Frances, on the other hand, determined long ago that by intentionally realigning just twenty minutes of less-than-productive time each day into high-impact minutes, she is buying back eighty-three hours each year (based on a five-day work week and fifty-week work year). This is the equivalent of over two forty-hour work weeks of added productive activity annually, without her ever having to put in a single additional hour of time at work. Her next goal is to find another twenty minutes per day—every two minutes here and five minutes there quickly adds to twenty—she can upgrade into more productive time.

BIG Bullet: A day is not maximized whose minutes have been marginalized.

BIG Questions: If your daily routine were filmed and sold as a training tool for greater success, how much would it be worth? What can you do to make it a blockbuster?

4. I MAKE PRODUCTIVE USE OF MY DOWNTIME AND COMMUTE.

Downtime (your time at work or home with nothing specifically scheduled to do) and commute can make up a substantial chunk of your life. It is time that, depending on how you invest it, can either give you an edge or nudge you into complacency. Does what you do in that time make your *WHY* more attainable? Or does your use of downtime create obstacles that can stall or reverse your progress, making your *WHY* less attainable? Frank broke the habit of listening each Monday to sports talk radio on the way to work, as he would often arrive angry after hearing commentators diss his favorite team or players. The fact he yelled at the radio only worsened his focus and wasted energy. It is common for people with minimal intentionality in their life to web surf, channel surf, wait, or sleep through irreplaceable hours each week: hours they could have used to shape up mentally or physically, read, build relationships, converse with family, plan, think, study, practice, pray, rejuvenate, and more.

Becoming more intentional and rigorous with your downtime is about being aware, not anal. It is not having every moment of your life scheduled in advance, but more importantly understanding how to take small or large blocks of time and exchange what you do that is less than optimal in those blocks in favor of something more productive—thereby putting that time to work for you instead of against you.

Frank Mitigates the Misery

Frank hates going to the dentist, but a tip he picked up from Frances makes his visits there less miserable. Rather than further intensify an already tense situation by watching the horrors of world news on CNN in the waiting room—right before the stress of having metal drilled into his mouth—he reviews the goals he has logged in the Notes app of his phone and converts unproductive downtime into a brief and effective motivational session. He does the same thing when waiting to board a flight, standing in line, and more.

While Frank would never admit it to Frances, once weekly during his twenty-minute commute time he has also started listening to a motivational podcast he heard her mention. While he still opts to listen to the news on other days, he has noticed that it is harder to get focused when he arrives to work after enduring what is less than inspiring and normally finds himself discussing what he heard with other team members, making everyone within earshot momentarily less productive.

BIG Bullet: While you cannot get more time, you can redeem what you have already for something more productive and positive.

BIG Questions: How much downtime do you spend weekly in your commute? How many hours of television do you take in each night? How much of this will you redeem for activities more aligned with your *WHY*?

5. I BUDGET TIME TO IMPROVE.

Life does not improve you by accident. Learning, like so much that is worthwhile in life, cannot be left to chance: You must again move from incidental to intentional. This means that one of the daily priorities discussed earlier in this chapter should be to budget or set aside time to yourself. How or what you choose to improve is up to you; *that* you do it each day is not an option if you want to build your capacity for killer instinct and mental toughness, and steadily close the gap between where you are and where you aspire to be.

Frances used to believe that attending training with a great attitude and applying its lessons demonstrated optimal teachability. She later discovered it was also what she did on her own, budgeting time to improve in between those meetings, that propelled her to an entirely different level.

BIG Bullet: To become intentionally great you must work as rigorously on yourself as you do on your job.

BIG Questions: Do you have a monthly intentional growth program to work on a specific skill, habit, or attitude? If you currently have one, when is the last time you took it up a notch and raised your basis? If you do not have one, do you believe that committing to intentional growth might just accelerate your success exponentially?

6. I MAKE TIME TO ADD VALUE TO OTHERS.

If the external category of your *WHY* includes helping or adding value to others—and it should—moving toward more intentionality and setting aside time to make this happen every day, if even in some small way, is a necessity. Just because you are spending time with someone does not mean you are adding value to them. In fact, depending on how you spend your time, you could be unwittingly subtracting value and leaving them worse off than when you encountered them. Impact best happens with intent: making time to encourage, equip, share, help, listen to, mentor, and coach other people. You are also likely to discover that adding value to others each day has a reciprocal effect, because the people you are impacting will in return challenge, stretch, and refine you in a way that makes you more valuable.

BIG Bullet: When one candle lights another, it does not diminish its own light; it multiplies it.

BIG Question: What impact could you have if you set a goal to intentionally impact at least three people daily through instructive or encouraging texts, conversations, emails, or training/coaching/mentoring?

7. I FOCUS MORE ON KEY ACTIVITIES THAN OUTCOMES.

Though at first glance this aspect may sound like a repeat of point 1 (schedule your priorities), it in fact broadens that point in three ways.

First, key activities are not strictly limited to the handful of priorities you had scheduled for workplace performance but include other important actions extending into all of life's sectors as well:

- Making the first move to apologize to a spouse even though the desired outcome—completely restored marital harmony—may not be evident for some time to come.
- Weighing in after dieting with discipline for ten days only to realize you gained two pounds, yet deciding to trust the process with the belief that the outcome will take care of itself as long as you keep doing the right things.
- While not yet seeing any immediate correlation between an online course you are taking and actual results, you persist with your learning, knowing you are building a deeper knowledge foundation that will pay massive dividends throughout your future.

BIG Bullet: Don't confuse the scoreboard for the game.

Furthermore, this aspect includes your second- and third-tier tasks as well as your scheduled priorities. These may not be the priorities, the best things, but they are still high-leverage actions you must perform daily with excellence and consistency to regain, sustain, or increase progress and growth.

Lastly, this aspect emphasizes that evaluating a day's success on outcomes should occur secondarily. Primarily you will measure the day's success on the key activities you engaged in throughout your rigorous daily routine that are most predictive of creating the right outcome.

A Harvest Reaped Versus Seeds Sown

Fred never considers a day a success unless he makes a sale. Through this lens he has far more unfulfilling days than rewarding ones. Frances, however, evaluates a day's effectiveness based on her success in executing, with excellence, the key actions most likely to create a sales outcome. She understands that on the days she makes several sales, many of those sales were set up by calls she made to customers days or weeks before. While the sale showed up on that particular day, it was not the result of something she did that day. Thus, even if she makes several sales that day but fails to execute the actions most likely to create future sales, she judges the day harshly, as her sales pipeline dried up to a degree. On the other hand, she evaluates days where she immerses herself in her highest-impact activities as a great success, even if no sales were made that day. She understands and believes in the power and process of consistent execution—grasping that it leads to sales over time, not overnight—and in so doing, lives Robert Louis Stevenson's words, "Don't judge each day by the harvest you reap but by the seeds that you plant."[30]

BIG Bullet: If the right activities create the outcomes, and they do, one must become more obsessed with right daily actions than the outcome itself. Execute the right game plan well and the scoreboard takes care of itself.

BIG Questions: Does it make sense to reevaluate what you declare as a "great day"? Can you see how some days with great outcomes have little to do with what you actually did that day but were perhaps set up on days when you engaged in right activities but didn't have a tangible outcome to show for it? Does it make sense that you should feel fulfilled on days you seem to have little results but are intentionally engaged in a rigorous daily routine and execute the necessary actions that eventually bring the outcomes to fulfill your *WHY*?

FIVE KEYS FOR RIGOR

Like all the ACCREDITED traits, rigor can be developed and improved. It requires the killer instinct to embrace structure, follow processes, and attack your stated priorities each day. It also mandates mental toughness so that when things get tough during the day, or you get off track, you can remain tenacious and resilient and complete them regardless. Let's go back to basics for a moment and discuss five keys that will ensure your killer instinct and mental toughness continue to grow so you can engage in more rigorous daily routines.

- **Keep your *WHY* clear and compelling.** After all, you need reasons to attack every day and to persist when you encounter setbacks, delays, frustrations, or defeats.
- **Execute your mindset routine.** Your morning mindset routine must be effective and consistent because it will help you focus on what your priorities are and guide you to avoid or minimize the distractions that get you off track.
- **Be prepared and equipped.** You need the knowledge, training, and skill to execute your priorities well. It does you little good to be aware of your priorities but not be able to do them with excellence.
- **Hold yourself accountable.** Making excuses for yourself or blaming others or other things for a failure to do what is most essential each day is a false kindness you grant yourself that relieves immediate pressure but creates long-term denial and underperformance.
- **Run the game film.** Spend time at the end of the day running the mental game film of the day and recognize where you did well, why you were able to do it well, and how you can do it well again. Notice also where you got off track and why, and adjust so you do not repeat

the same error tomorrow. The Personal Progress Diary used during the ACCREDITED course will help you develop this habit.

BIG Bullet: "The unexamined life is not worth living."[31] —Socrates

INTENTIONAL ACTION

Consider your various life sector routines: workplace, health and exercise, study, practice, downtime, and more. Then evaluate how you can improve each routine by working more within the disciplines of priorities, changing those priorities, or executing them more consistently.

BADGERS ADVERSITY INCIDENT #8

January 24, 2020: Purdue Blows out the Badgers 70–51

Needing to recover and reestablish the momentum lost at Michigan State a week prior, the Badgers focused on taking down conference rival Purdue.

For the second time in a week the Badgers were battered by a conference rival. Purdue came out hot and the Badgers were unable to slow them down. With only six weeks left in the season, any modicum of momentum they hoped to gain was again squashed.

PLAY A POOR HAND WELL

- When conditions rage against you, do you become too passive while trying to weather the storm? With regard to decisions you can make or actions you can take, how can you shift your attitude to embrace the struggle and reverse the course of negative momentum when it works against you?

Chapter Nine

EFFORT

Work Harder Smarter and Smarter Harder

People are fond of evaluating their and others' work ethics based on the total number of hours or days they are at work instead of whether they are doing the most effective things intelligently and with vigor during those hours and days. We see this principle applied to hours spent not just in the workplace, but elsewhere, such as the gym, a house of worship, a classroom, and more. Working harder smarter means doing the right things with excellence and continually finding ways to improve them. Working smarter harder is about giving complete attention and effort to those high-impact activities, rather than doing them well but half-heartedly.

In the workplace, for instance, a consequence of failing to work harder smarter and smarter harder is that you must often work longer, trying to get done what you could have accomplished in less time had you worked harder on the right things and done them excellently. While there are times when you must put in the extra hours and days of work to accomplish a specific goal or task—or based on situational needs of an organization—the goal is to maximize one's time and effort while in the workplace. In doing so, you can eventually spend less additional time there, redirecting that time into pursuing more balance in your life as you channel a killer instinct and mental toughness to accomplish your *WHY* in areas outside of your vocation: family, fitness, relationships, spirituality, social or charitable causes, and more.

BIG Bullet: An intentional mindset catalyzes smarter, harder effort.

What's Put in the Hours Versus the Hours Put In

Amy, Frances's special-needs daughter, is the most meaningful aspect of her *WHY*. For Frances, time spent with Amy is not an either-or proposition of quality versus quantity—she prioritizes both. To accomplish this, Frances must fully maximize the time she spends at work so that she does not have to put in overtime or work days off to meet her goals; she must employ daily rigor and demonstrate a work ethic that prioritizes working harder smarter and smarter harder. To this end she enters the workplace with her priorities already scheduled and her day well planned.

Before even setting out for work, she reviews her plan as part of her morning mindset routine. This level of focus allows her to avoid starting the day in neutral. The heightened awareness of her daily nonnegotiable activities that comes from reviewing her plan likewise enables her to stay mentally checked in to the vital tasks at hand—despite disappointments or distractions she encounters that are beyond her control—and more quickly recognize and correct her course if she gets off track.

Frank considers himself a quick thinker, nimble innovator, and improviser. Because of this he takes pride in being able to accomplish more than most of his coworkers without having a specific plan, operating instead out of instinct and making the most of whatever comes at him each day. He fails to realize his success comes *despite* the fact he is not working harder smarter and smarter harder, not *because* of that reality.

Even when Fred is far behind his sales quota he will not work additional time to make up lost ground as the month progresses. He is fond of saying, "I want to have a life" and "Life is more than just work." Because he does not possess a *WHY* that would compel him to do otherwise, he works neither hard nor smart nor long, and his perpetually pathetic results show it. Fred makes the mistake of many in confusing "having a life" with having a banal existence, as he brings the same lack of intentionality exhibited at work to life's other arenas as well, often being out of shape physically, relationally, mentally, and spiritually.

BIG Bullet: The objective of being anywhere is to fully *be there*, to completely engage with what and who matters most at the moment.

SEVEN KEY ASPECTS OF EFFORT

1. I DO ALL THAT I CAN WITHOUT HOLDING BACK.

This aspect pertains specifically to your vocation and bringing all that you can in your role day in and day out. Here are a few considerations to keep in mind when evaluating this aspect:

- how much unnecessary time you spent in idle, nonwork-related conversations: politics, sports, world events, and more
- how much unnecessary time you spent eating at work (It is not uncommon for people to arrive at work, clock in, and then sit down to eat breakfast! This is *not* working at work. Eat before work or at given lunch and break times, but not during work time because the objective of being at work is to work harder smarter and smarter harder—not to eat more food more often!)

- how much nonrelated, personal business you conducted at work (This includes phone calls, texts, emails, checking stock portfolios, checking on social media, perusing nonwork-related websites, and more.)

Pacer Versus Racer

Months ago, in a meeting the team well remembers, the sales manager, Alex, was trying to rally Fred, Frank, Frances, and their seven teammates to give it all they had at work without holding back so they could finish the month strong and surpass their goals.

"We're not paying anyone to come in each day, take up space, and pace themselves or budget their efforts," Alex declared. "Everyone is expected to step up and give all they have, every day."

After squirming through Alex's call for more effort, Fred, sure the remarks were at least in part directed at him, replied defensively, "I can't buy into that. I do pace myself and I don't regret it because I'm in this for the long haul, and I don't want to burn out."

Alex looked at Fred in stunned amusement and cocked his head, saying, "Fred, how can you burn out when you've never been on fire?"

Fred sat speechless as Alex continued, "I promise you that you're in no danger of burning out. Your pace hasn't served you very well the past couple years. How about picking it up a bit and seeing how that works out for you instead?"

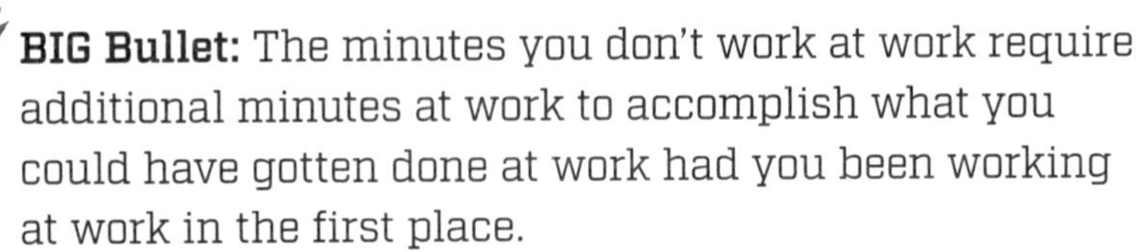

BIG Bullet: The minutes you don't work at work require additional minutes at work to accomplish what you could have gotten done at work had you been working at work in the first place.

BIG Question: What can you do to make your *WHY* so meaningful that you do not give yourself the option not to work at work?

2. I EXECUTE THE MOST ESSENTIAL TASKS.

As addressed in the previous chapter, effective execution is not just about getting a lot done, but getting the right things done. Bear in mind the following questions when working to improve this aspect:

- Did I execute the task half-heartedly or with complete effort?
- Did I rush through it—do it just to do it—or spend adequate time on it?
- As my goal is to continually compete with my former self, did I find a way to improve my ability to do the task, if even in a small way?
- Have my priorities changed to a point where this is a task I should no longer prioritize or perhaps not even do at all?

BIG Bullet: Doing more of the wrong things well, and often, cannot be declared as progress.

BIG Question: Do you tend to do the most essential tasks just to do them or to do them with excellence and consistency daily?

3. I RAISE MY BASIS.

You may recall from chapter three a discussion on changing or raising your basis as a method for building mental toughness. Your basis is any routine that, while productive, does not challenge you as much as it once did because you have mastered it. Raising your basis involves increasing the most productive activities within a routine. Changing your basis relates to lessening or eliminating altogether the number of unproductive activities you engage in, or the amount of time you spend on them (for example, reducing your intake of television from two hours to ninety minutes per day). In both cases, you will need to fight through the discomfort of disrupting what you are used to, which is a catalyst for growth.

When you increase the amount of harder and smarter effort you put forth, while simultaneously reducing the actions that are unproductive, you win in at least three ways: You upgrade killer instinct, you increase mental toughness, and you maximize more moments and days.

Cold Shower Catalyst

Frances is relentless in finding ways to disrupt her comfortable personal and work routines, even in small or seemingly unorthodox ways. She knows the ensuing discomfort heightens her alertness, urgency, and mental toughness. Recently, Frances has started employing a technique she first heard on a Navy SEAL podcast that described how showering in cold water early in the morning disrupts one's comfort zone; creates focus, urgency, and alertness; and even builds confidence as you gradually, over time, increase the time spent in leaving the water cold. After a solid week that began initially with an excruciating fifteen seconds that seemed like five minutes, she is now up to a full minute of cold showering before letting the hot water rule. In Frances's mind, the cold water keeps her out of hot water by combating complacency first thing in the morning.

BIG Bullet: What most people call eccentric, winners call effective.

BIG Questions: In which of your life's routines have you changed your basis since reading chapter three? Which basis will you change next? Are you up for the cold-water challenge?

4. I INVEST EFFORT IN MY GROWTH.

In the last chapter I presented the aspect "I budget time to improve," which focused on setting aside time to intentionally work on yourself. This particular aspect evaluates whether you used well the time you set aside or applied only minimal effort. For instance, if you read a book, did you underline and highlight key passages, and perhaps transpose the notes into a Word document to make reviewing your takeaways more effective in the future? If you took an online course, did you focus fully and resist the temptation to minimize the screen and surf other sites to check social media, the stock market, news headlines, or sports scores? Incidentally, this aspect includes matters we have discussed previously like your morning mindset routine and using the Personal Progress Diary at day's end to evaluate the trait aspects you are working on. To sum up this aspect, did you go beyond budgeting time to improve and give all you had to the time you budgeted?

BIG Bullet: There is no question that getting better takes time, but the time will pass regardless. The question is, will time just age you or improve you?

BIG Questions: What was the last personal development course you took or serious book you read? What did you like best about it, what were some of the key principles it shared, and what have you applied or changed as a result of reading it?

5. I DON'T SPEND MAJOR TIME ON MINOR THINGS.

Spending major time on minor things is like eating unhealthy foods. You may never eliminate all of it from your diet, but to perform better you must limit your intake. When evaluating living out this aspect, awareness is key because it will help you take the bait less often and return to the track more quickly when you do. Here is a sampling of "minor" things prone to rob our time if we let them:

- conversations about matters you cannot control
- conversations that have nothing to do with moving you toward your *WHY*
- tasks you should delegate or outsource
- engaging in mindless television or radio programs
- things you may enjoy doing but are low return and sap precious time from priorities
- things you may enjoy doing but are destructive to do
- obsessive social media engagement
- overall media engagement
- sleeping in too much or too often
- gaming binges
- various vice indulgences
- giving time to everyone asking for it
- aimless web or channel surfing
- spending too much time with people who make you feel worse about yourself
- spending too much time with people you do not want to become like

A key to evaluating your success with this aspect will have much to do with how you gauge "major time." With a higher regard for your irreplaceable time, you may wish to classify major time as a matter of minutes. Even a minute or two at a time poorly invested repeatedly throughout the day can amount to substantial unproductive moments that could have been used more intentionally and effectively.

BIG Bullet: Time is maximized when you invest bigger blocks of it into smaller numbers of high-impact tasks and people.

BIG Questions: Throughout your day, where are you prone to spend the most time with tasks or people that have nothing to do with taking you to your *WHY*—making the journey longer because of the distractions they create and energy they drain? Where can you intentionally realign that time into something that matters more?

6. I SAY "NO" TO LOW-RETURN THINGS.

Though the previous aspect concerned limiting the amount of time you spend unproductively, this aspect doubles down and raises the stakes, evaluating your ability to not engage in low-return things at all. These can be former activities or bad habits you overlook, walk away from, and renounce or avoid altogether. Consider trying the following:

- canceling a subscription to amusing but unproductive publications or other media services
- unsubscribing to unproductive emails that you waste time deleting each day
- not responding to or joining the countless political or sports debates on social media
- restraining yourself from punitive horn-blowing to let people know what you think of their driving decisions
- ignoring the temptation to trade one insult for another and instead moving on to something more productive
- grabbing your coffee and getting back to work rather than hanging around to listen to the latest team grievances or gossip
- not doing the unproductive things others are doing just to fit in with them or appear nonjudgmental
- refusing a seat on a board or committee that might flatter your ego but require too much time

Frances Throws in the Towel

When Frances joined the company as the only female salesperson, she naturally wanted to fit in and be accepted and liked. She gave audience to the complaints, gossip, and whining that normally followed each meeting—the so called "meeting after the meeting." She did not defend Alex when her teammates would privately criticize him for pushing them hard and expecting too much. She was reluctant to admit she enjoyed the company training sessions while others grumbled about attending them. In short, she let the crowd compromise her, and it left her feeling dishonest and untrue to herself. So, one day she gave it all up. She did not make a formal announcement or condemn others for how unproductive they were. She decided instead to let her better example be her explanation and stopped putting herself into situations that prioritized getting along over getting better. Did she still care about the team? Of course! In fact, she cared enough to not enable their nonsensical tendencies and to set a higher standard for aspiring to instead.

BIG Bullet: Maturity is mastering the art of avoidance and escape: to avoid what is unproductive whenever possible and to escape when it is thrust upon you.

BIG Question: What mindset, tendency, activity, or habit must you work to eliminate from your daily routine, and perhaps from your life altogether, that is preventing you from working harder smarter and smarter harder?

7. I GIVE ALL-OUT EFFORT IN MY VARIOUS LIFE ARENAS: FAMILY, EXERCISE, AND SO ON.

Whereas the first aspect of this trait concerned your effort at work, this aspect is directed to your various life roles away from work, for any area you want to measurably and continually improve in your life requires an intentional mindset just as it does at work. The same principles apply: prioritizing, engaging in, giving to, and getting from the moment, not just getting through it. This means raising your effort in areas such as:

- competing with your former self as a parent, spouse, or friend.
- consistently changing your basis in workout, eating, personal growth, and financial and spiritual disciplines.
- mastering the art of engagement. Engagement is about emotional investment, so fully engage wherever you are. When you are on vacation, *be there*; do not check work emails hourly. When you are spending time with your children, *be there*; do not diminish your conversations by glancing at social media. When you are at the gym, *be there* and work out; do not watch others, flirt with attendants, or pose at every mirror you pass. If you are taking an educational course, *be there* and ask questions, do your homework, record notes, and apply what you learn; do not just get through it, get from it.

The Hard-to-Please Papa

In chapter two I introduced Frank's desire to win the long-sought approval of his high-achieving dad as an essential aspect of his *WHY*. For years, Frank's focus has been to go all out in impressing his dad with how he has matured, what he has learned, his success at work, and his financial progress. To Frank's credit, he recognized that while this complete effort was well-intended, it was not working. Frank Sr. seemed indifferent and at times even bored by Frank's self-serving efforts.

While Frank's goal in this endeavor has not changed, his method has. Where in past encounters he would do most of the talking, trying to impress his dad with his life, he decided to shift his attentions to try harder to understand and learn about his dad—to show his dad he cared more about him as a person than about impressing him as a son. Frank started asking more questions about his dad's journey, what he had done, lessons he had learned, as well as about his health and future aspirations. He is now moving from a son who wanted to compete against his dad financially to one who wants a more robust relationship with him. Frank is learning the wisdom in author and motivator Zig Ziglar's words, "While I like the things money can buy, I love what money won't buy."[32]

BIG Bullet: When effort misses the target, do not blame the bull's-eye. Do improve your aim.

LITTLE LETUPS VERSUS LITTLE BIT EXTRA

People let up a little because they allow themselves that option. Others do all they can, and then some, because that is the only option they give themselves. In either case one's thinking (more than skills, knowledge, talent, or experience) will determine one's course. And, in the event I failed in past chapters to make clear what significantly influences one's mindset moment by moment, let me reiterate in no uncertain terms: It is one's *WHY*. A weak *WHY* allows letups while a bold and compelling *WHY* makes them out of the question and mandates giving that little bit extra even when you are tired, when you do not feel like giving it, or when you are not seeing immediate results.

For a closing dose of perspective on this chapter, consider these thoughts: Working smarter harder and harder smarter is not punishment. It is, however, an intentional, richly rewarding lifestyle that endows the doer with levels of self-esteem, self-confidence, killer instinct, and mental toughness that are unattainable to those content to do just enough or who occasionally extend themselves, but only when it suits them.

BIG Questions: Have you considered how letups in one of life's arenas might negatively impact another? For instance, if you are out of shape physically, can that affect your relationships? If your relationships are toxic, might that impact your health? If you have become stale mentally, will it diminish your workplace performance?

INTENTIONAL ACTION

List each of what you consider as your key life arenas: vocation, school, athletics, immediate family, extended family, significant other, friendships, health/exercise, spirituality, personal growth, finances, and the like. Can you find one intentional step you can take in each arena listed to improve your aim with more strategic actions, enhance your focus, increase your effort, or change your basis?

BADGERS ADVERSITY INCIDENT #9

January 26, 2020: Second-Leading Scorer on the Badgers Abruptly Quits the Team

Desperately trying to finish January strong before heading into the final seven weeks of the season, the Badgers sought to regroup and earn a win in the upcoming game against Iowa.

Shortly after the blowout loss to Purdue, the Badgers' leading shot taker and second-leading scorer caught the struggling team and staff by surprise by abruptly quitting the team. The Badgers would now have to finish the remainder of the season undermanned and would need to adjust to compensate for a loss of talent and firepower.

PLAY A POOR HAND WELL

- What do you do to keep your own focus and motivation and uplift others when adverse conditions pile on you one after another, others give up on you, others walk out of your life, or others write you off as a lost cause?
- How can you prevent the actions or attitudes of others toward you from defining you? How can you use their dismissal of you as wood on the fire of your *WHY*? If others have more talent than you, how can you increase your toughness to give you an edge?

Chapter Ten

DISCIPLINE

Become a No-Nonsense Master of "No'ing"

Discipline has several definitions, but ultimately, and unfortunately, the word can evoke a negative connotation: "That kid needs to be disciplined," "I'm going to discipline you," "the pain of discipline," and the like. Despite that discipline can sound like a punishing and restricting force that saps joy from your life, the opposite is true. To fit the context of this chapter, discipline can be best defined as an activity, regimen, or exercise that improves a skill, habit, or attitude. For a healthier and refreshing perspective on discipline, let's look at some of its outstanding attributes.

- **Discipline is freedom.** When you make yourself do the things you must do, the day comes when you can do the things you want to do.
- **Discipline is a morale builder.** You feel better about yourself when you do the right thing the right way, especially when you did not feel like doing it but did it anyway.
- **Discipline bridges the gap between where you are and where you aspire to be.** Whereas decisions (as mentioned in chapter four) get you started, discipline helps you finish. The discipline to act begins converting your intention into a result.

- **Discipline gives you better and more (not fewer) options over the course of your lifetime.** Discipline often amounts to giving up what you want now (overcoming instant gratification) for what you want most. The more disciplined you are with your money now through budgeting and investing, the *more* options you have later in life. The greater your health disciplines now, you will have *more*, not fewer, options of activities to engage in as you age. The discipline you apply to personal growth now increases your options for helping others, making decisions, solving problems, innovating, and more.
- **Discipline builds right habits and fuels consistency.** Habits are actions you have done so often, because of discipline, they become automatic. From these habits, consistency ensues.
- **Discipline is a separator between the many with marginal and the modicum with major levels of killer instinct and mental toughness.** Discipline steels you to continue attacking your goals and to fight through the obstacles standing between you and them. It causes you to do and stick with what is uncomfortable, raising your self-confidence, self-esteem, and basis.

BIG Bullet: No champion in any endeavor credited being undisciplined as their secret to success.

DISCIPLINE LIMITS UNPRODUCTIVE OPTIONS

Once you define and embolden your *WHY*, it is easier to know what you must prioritize—what to say "yes" to—each day. Once those priorities are established up front, you are also clearer on what you must say "no" to—the unproductive options that derail your progress or unnecessarily lengthen your journey. "No" is a wonderful word, and highly disciplined people are "Masters of No'ing," precisely because they first decided what must be done daily to move them toward their goals: "No, don't have time for that"; "Nope, I'm not going to get involved in that"; "No, I can't commit to that" . . . why? "Because I have these other priorities I am working on right now." "No" is a complete sentence, by the way. It says it all; you do not need to rationalize or explain.

You are more likely to develop and stick with disciplines after you have clarified your *WHY*, because you must have compelling reasons to do certain things well and consistently that you may not want to do, while saying no to things you might enjoy but are counterproductive. This validates the fact that discipline can be developed; it is neither genetic nor is it something anyone else can force within you. You can build it within yourself by first deciding what it is in life you want most and resolving to pay the price to get it. In this respect, building an intentional mindset is a chief ally and catalyst for discipline.

BIG Bullet: Mastering one's self precedes conquering one's goals.

SEVEN KEY ASPECTS OF DISCIPLINE

1. I EXECUTE MY PRE-WORK MINDSET AND/OR EXERCISE ROUTINE.

Executing your pre-work mindset routine—tuning and sharpening up your mindset before you are at work and before it comes under attack during the course of a day's events—can be as simple as reviewing your *WHY*, reading or reciting affirmations, examining your priorities for the day, or listening to or reading something inspirational or motivational. In terms of exercise, it's challenging yourself to finish strong on the last rep of a structured set and resist the urge to rack the weight early, saying, "That's good enough for today." While this point focuses on your intentional mindset and exercise/health regimens, it can include any of the essential routines you have previously held or were inspired to establish after reading chapter eight on the trait of rigor.

BIG Bullet: Executing routines, or not, either pays you or pains you throughout the day. The pain of discipline pays you back. The pain of regret haunts you for life.

BIG Questions: Are there any important routines you do not currently have that you must start? Are there routines you once had that you must return to? Do you have a current routine that must be tweaked for relevance or executed with more consistency and/or excellence?

2. I EXECUTE COMMITMENTS REGARDLESS OF HOW I FEEL.

Allow me to pose a few questions to you concerning the days you do not feel like executing your vital routines or keeping commitments you made to yourself or others:

- *So what* if you don't feel like doing it?
- What do your feelings have to do with whether you do what is right?
- Why should you allow how you momentarily feel to determine whether you do what can change your life permanently?

In addition to the numerous rewards of doing what is essential when you do not feel like it, here is one that is often overlooked: When you don't feel like executing key tasks or keeping other commitments but decide to do it nonetheless, you will feel even better about yourself than on the days you wanted to do them. Discipline is not a form of punishment, but a morale builder.

The Last Time for Frances

The last time Frances skipped her morning mindset routine was the last time Frances skipped her morning mindset routine. Feeling less than 100 percent physically, she slept in through the time she had allotted each morning to review her *WHY*, her daily priorities, and her affirmations. She reasoned in the moment that her body needed more attention than her mind. But as her physical condition worsened throughout the day, she recognized that becoming more mentally focused and energized could have positively influenced her physically. Frances's story reminds us that even tough people have weak moments.

BIG Bullet: Soft people live life feeling their way into acting. Mentally tough people develop the discipline to act their way into feeling. They will not let feelings derail their future.

Don't Just Do It to Do It!

On Fred's day off he technically kept the commitment he made to his wife to clean the garage: doing what he said he would and when he said he would do it. He did not feel like doing it. He did not like doing it. And he does not even feel better now that it is done. Why? He did it just to do it, with the wrong attitude.

For instance, when he could not pull himself away from college football games, his wife had to remind him three times to get moving. His ABLE was poor and he complained the whole time he did it, saying things like, "Who used this last?" "Why can't anyone ever put anything back where it belongs?" "Why'd you waste money on junk like this?" and, "I can't believe I'm sweeping up dirt when I should be watching Alabama take on Auburn."

He did a mediocre job, saying to himself, "This is good enough for now. At least it's better than it was. I'll do that corner next week."

If the virtue category of Fred's *WHY* included traits to improve like attention to detail, attitude, servant's mindset, and developing discipline, he would have approached this mundane task with the mindset to make his garage a masterpiece.

To truly enjoy and benefit the most from the fruits of your discipline, make up your mind that if you are going to keep a commitment or execute a routine, you give it all you have, do it with a great attitude, and consider all tasks—whether small or large—as a reflection of your own personal standards and brand.

BIG Bullet: Ultimately, how you do anything is how you do everything because all things you do reflect the same mindset.

BIG Questions: What priorities in your personal or work life are you prone to skip on the days you do not feel like doing them? What about your *WHY* must you decide to crave more so that skipping it in the future is no longer an option?

3. I SAY "NO" TO SHORTCUTS AND INSTANT GRATIFICATION.

As suggested in this chapter's opening paragraphs, this exercise becomes much easier once you have become resolutely clear as to what you must say "yes" to each day. We truly live in an age that worships at the altar of instant "everything," including instant gratification. Because of this, developing the discipline to control your ABLE, stick with a rigorous daily routine, work harder smarter and smarter harder, and the like can set you apart more than ever before.

One reason people do unproductive things like putting in minimal effort, improvising through their day, making a character compromise, wasting too much time, shortcutting or skipping prescribed processes, and the like, is because they see no immediate negative consequence for their actions. Because they are slack or sloppy and nothing seemingly dire happens, they are prone to repeat the behavior again and again until the wrong action has become a habit lethal to their growth.

BIG Bullet: The more often you repeat an unproductive behavior the more it starts to feel normal. The more it feels normal the less conscious you are of the impact and its consequences.

Hope as you may, there is no escaping the reality that repeated undisciplined actions will catch up with you—not always overnight, but certainly over time. This is because our actions have a compounding effect, regardless of whether they are productive or unproductive. Just as productive actions do not always show an immediate result but will over time if you continue them, the same compounding principle applies to unproductive decisions and actions.

They *will* catch up to you.

You *are not* the exception.

You have now been warned.

BIG Bullet: When you find yourself in a rut, it is not the result of an action you took last night, but it reflects a series of failed decisions and disciplines sown over time that have come home to roost.

BIG Questions: In which areas of your life are you most prone to forgo the harder, longer, inconvenient, and costly route, and take the bait for what is easier, cheaper, quicker, and more enjoyable—knowing full well it is not what is best for you? What must change for you to trade in what is fast or fun in the moment for what is fulfilling and effective over a lifetime?

4. I SPEND LESS TIME WITH UNDISCIPLINED "SURFING."

Have you ever turned your head from an important task for just a moment to have it become an hour, or even evolve into most of the day? Or perhaps you have had that flirtation with a new Netflix show, Spotify station, Food Network series, unproductive website, or social media obsession dominate the rest of your week? If something like this has happened to you at work or at home, you have got plenty of company—unproductive company.

Fred's Day at the Ballpark

Fred was given a written reprimand for the first time during his two-year tenure with the company after a day he spent at the ballpark. The problem was that he watched the game at work. His undisciplined surfing started as an occasional reviewing of the afternoon scores on his office computer under the guise of updating customer files. Before long he was taking in entire innings at a time. Fred rationalized that watching the games made his job more fulfilling and less stressful and would thus have a positive effect on his work performance. He failed to consider that management's monthly audit of employee browsing history would raise red flags. While he was embarrassed by his write-up, he was relieved he had not yet started visiting the online gaming site he had heard so much about.

BIG Bullet: "Starve your distractions, feed your focus."[33] —Daniel Goleman

BIG Questions: Do you tend to minimize the impact of "surfing" tendencies on your *WHY*, killer instinct, and mental toughness? Do you rationalize frequent or excessive surfing as harmless or as a release that adds balance in your life? Does it make sense that if your

WHY were more compelling in all life's vital arenas, it would not allow you the option of consistently spending time in this manner?

5. I SAY "NO" TO EXCESSIVE TRIVIAL PURSUITS, IDLE CONVERSATION, AND WAITING/WISHING/WHINING.

While the prior aspect had to do with undisciplined surfing, for this point you will be working on limiting or eliminating undisciplined speech with a heavy emphasis on:

- **pursuing or listening to gossip.** If you discuss other people, especially concerning rumors, speculation, or other unconfirmed details, you are a gossip. If you listen to this nonsense, you become a gossip by enabling it. Nothing productive comes from gossip. It dilutes your focus, damages your character, drains your energy, dings your attitude, and wastes irreplaceable time.
- **conversations that have nothing to do with building relationships, impacting others, becoming a better person, or working toward your *WHY*.** While there is likely to always be some degree of small talk between people in the workplace, it can get out of hand. Be more aware of the quality and length of these conversations and consider whether what you are talking about is taking you closer to your *WHY* or making it tougher to get there. If it is the latter, cut it short and move on.
- **whining or complaining.** Whining and complaining are common traits of mentally soft people, unfocused people, and those with little regard for the time or the productivity of those around them. Quite frankly, people who have built an intentional mindset and are laser-locked on their *WHY* do not have time for this foolishness. They understand that engaging in whining or complaining makes them, and everyone who hears them, momentarily less productive.
- **discussing your personal problems with anyone your problem does not concern or involve.** Be more selective with whom you

> discuss your personal problems: relationship issues, marriage matters, health ailments, financial struggles, frustrations with your kids, and the like. It helps to realize that everyone else you are sharing them with also has their own set of challenges they are working through. If too many people know too much about you, it is time to develop more awareness and discipline in selecting your speech.

Many people think their mouth is their own worst enemy: The things they say, and the way they say them, get them in trouble, isolate them, cost them relationships, knock them off track, and regularly make themselves and everyone else miserable. But the mouth is not the core issue; the heart is. What is in one's heart comes out of one's mouth. This is why character is an ACCREDITED trait, and why virtue reasons—the kind of person you wish to become—are a key component of your *WHY*. You are not likely to measurably improve your discipline, character, or language without an intentional mindset, effort, or adjustments. It takes work. Lots of it. Over time. Stay after it. It is worth it because learning to shift your mouth out of overdrive and into neutral more often will change your life.

Frank Steps Up

When Frances first joined the team and began beating Frank's sales every month, he handled it like a child, insulting her and gossiping about her—all in private, of course. But over time, her consistency and professionalism earned his respect. The last time Fred brought up an issue he had with Frances in conversation, Frank held up his hand and said, "Fred, instead of talking about Frances, perhaps you should go talk to her." Fred looked shocked and felt betrayed. With the conversation cut short, both Fred and Frank returned to more productive tasks.

BIG Bullet: If what you are going to say will not improve on the silence, leave the silence alone.

BIG Questions: Which of the points listed, if any, tend to cause you the most problems? Would it help you to intentionally wait three seconds before initiating or jumping into a conversation where you engage in these actions, and during those three seconds reflexively ask yourself, "Will what I'm going to say make me better or worse as a person and in my performance?"

6. I GET OFF TRACK LESS OFTEN THAN YESTERDAY.

Despite our best efforts to develop discipline and intentionality in words and deeds, we will still get off track from time to time. That is neither the point nor the question. The challenge is to *do it less often*. Since perfection is beyond our grasp, our goal is to gauge our growth by our ability to minimize imperfections and to celebrate the little victories: handling a single situation better than you would have yesterday, a week, or a year ago. Where we get stuck and regress is in repeating the same errors and digging the same holes to crawl out of day after day, year after year, decade after decade. If this is true for you, it is time to ramp up your competitive spirit and wage it more relentlessly on your former self.

As obvious as it sounds, the key to getting off track less often is to be completely clear about what the track is in the first place! Having a rigorous daily routine, scheduled priorities, deciding up front what you must say yes and no to, and so much else we have discussed in these pages is essential. It builds a foundation that increases awareness when you have strayed so you can quickly return to being productive again.

Frances's Post-It Note Nudge

When Frances started with the company eighteen months ago, she posted an eleven-word note on her computer that provoked mocking from teammates. They thought it was silly, amateurish, and unnecessary. Throughout her fifteen-month run as sales champ the note has remained. The mocking? That stopped a year ago. Here is what the note says: "*Am I doing the most productive thing possible at this moment?*"

The fact it is on the computer is strategically intentional. And Fred was willing to attest to that after his day at the ballpark earned him a written reprimand.

BIG Bullet: Success consists of going from failure to failure without loss of enthusiasm."[34]
—Winston Churchill

BIG Questions: What do you think of Frances's note? Is there a version of this awareness tool you can implement in your own daily routine to help you stay on track more often?

7. I STAY OFF TRACK FOR LESS TIME THAN YESTERDAY.

A key area for competition with your former self is improving your ability to course correct faster. We aspire not only to get off track less often but also to increase our awareness so that when it happens we do not stay off track as long. Anyone and everyone can, and will, get off track, but without an intentional mindset not anyone or everyone gets back on the right track expediently. In fact, it is common for some to stay off track so long they dig a rut and decline. The process of evaluating this aspect for seven consecutive days during the follow-up ACCREDITED course will jumpstart or accelerate your awareness in this regard. Staying on the track you have established to reach your *WHY* is such a high-stake action that improving this discipline will do no less than change your life.

BIG Bullet: Embrace failure. Missteps and roadblocks are inevitable but are ultimately an opportunity to learn, pivot, and go after your goals with new perspective."[35]
—Jenny Fleiss

BIG Questions: Since we all develop blind spots or are too close to issues to quickly recognize our flaws, would you be willing to give someone in your life permission to call you out when you are off track in words or actions? And when they do so to promise not to make excuses or assault the messenger?

EMBRACE DISCIPLINE

In case what I have shared in this chapter is not enough to improve your attitude about discipline and encourage you to embrace it, the following folks have been good enough to help me out:[36]

> "We do today what they won't, so tomorrow we can accomplish what they can't."
>
> —Dwayne "The Rock" Johnson

> "Winners embrace hard work. They love the discipline of it, the trade-off they're making to win. Losers, on the other hand, see it as a punishment. And that's the difference."
>
> —Lou Holtz

> "Discipline is the soul of an army. It makes small numbers formidable; procures success to the weak, and esteem to all."
>
> —George Washington

> "A disciplined mind leads to happiness, and an undisciplined mind leads to suffering."
>
> —Dalai Lama

> "The successful person has the habit of doing the things failures don't like to do. They don't like doing them either necessarily. But their disliking is subordinated to the strength of their purpose."
>
> —E. M. Gray

> "The only discipline that lasts is self-discipline."
>
> —Bum Philips

> "Discipline is the refining fire by which talent becomes ability."
>
> —Roy L. Smith

> "With self-discipline, most anything is possible."
>
> —Theodore Roosevelt

INTENTIONAL ACTION

Knowing that giving yourself too many options dilutes discipline, in which aspects of your daily routine or downtime can you eliminate unproductive options and thus narrow your focus in a way that stimulates more discipline? Try to come up with at least two unproductive options you will no longer allow yourself to engage in or will minimize in both your work routine and downtime.

BADGERS ADVERSITY INCIDENT #10

January 27, 2020: Iowa Defeats the Badgers After Trailing by Twelve with Just Minutes Remaining

Despite losing their second-leading scorer the day before, the Badgers pulled together and rallied to lead Iowa, in Iowa, by twelve points with time running out.

Despite rallying together after the departure of a key player, the Badgers failed to close out yet another game they could have won.

PLAY A POOR HAND WELL

- How do you respond when you perform well for the majority of a day, week, month, or more, but the final outcome turns against you?
- How can you become more resilient and recover faster from setbacks of defeat? Do you have, or can you create, an affirmation to help you with this?

Chapter Eleven

INTELLIGENCE

Grow Your Smarts Before Stupidity Starts

The definition of intelligence, "the ability to acquire and apply knowledge and skills,"[37] explains why your intelligence is *not* fixed. It also makes clear why so many people are much of the time only "half intelligent." Anyone with the mental capacity to read this far into this book obviously has the means to acquire skills and knowledge. As they develop greater killer instinct and mental toughness, they are also likely to do a more complete job of living out the second half of the definition and "*apply* knowledge and skills." The reality that many underachievers are better at the former aspect of intelligence than the latter sadly qualifies them for the "half intelligent" observation previously made.

BIG Bullet: Life's biggest gap is the one between knowing and doing. Killer instinct and mental toughness help you close that gap.

YOU ALREADY HAVE WHAT IT TAKES

The chances are excellent that at this moment it would not be necessary for you to learn one new additional thing nor acquire a single extra skill to achieve better results with your workout program, with your diet, in your finances, in the workplace, in your relationships, and more. All you would need to do is a more consistent and excellent job of applying what you have already learned in these areas over the years but do poorly, inconsistently, or not at all. Any new skills you developed, old skills you improved, or further knowledge you gained would be a bonus but not a prerequisite for you to improve aspects of your life in which you have acquired knowledge and skills that are unapplied. Frankly, this is very exciting and encouraging news for us all!

THE TRUTH ABOUT STUPIDITY

The word *stupid* is often overused without a clear understanding of what it really means: lacking in common sense or intelligence.[38] What this definition tells us is that if we know what to do but fail to do it, we are not just being lazy, forgetful, or apathetic, but that what we are doing lacks common sense and is, thus, stupid! Now, if you do not know any better, lack adequate information, or have not had the training, then you suffer from ignorance, not stupidity. But for many people, that is not the case. They *do* know but don't *do*, and they will not grow to their potential until they become more intentional about doing more of what they know, learning better ways to do it, and doing it consistently. In this regard, no one can fix anyone else's "stupid" tendencies, but each of us can remedy those tendencies for ourselves. Applying principles from the last chapter on discipline will be particularly helpful.

BE CAREFUL; IT CAN GET WORSE

As bad as stupid sounds, it gets worse. A "moron" is defined as "a very stupid person."[39] This would indicate one who does not learn from the past, repeats the same errors, or stops growing altogether—a type of stupidity on speed skates. All of us do "stupid" things from time to time, but that does not necessarily mark us as a stupid person, until stupidity begins to dominate our actions. To improve, we must grow in intelligence, because life is tougher when we continually approach the stop sign of stupidity, hit the gas, and blow right through it into "Moron Meadows."

BIG Bullet: You will not grow or progress by repeating the same old stupid things. You can grow and progress doing new stupid things and learning from them. In fact, this ability is a mark of intelligence.

SEVEN KEY ASPECTS OF INTELLIGENCE

1. I ACQUIRE NEW KNOWLEDGE.

This aspect relates to the "acquiring" portion of intelligence. While there is knowledge you can gain in hundreds of areas, the purpose of developing this ACCREDITED trait, and the basis for your evaluating and grading it, will be in acquiring new knowledge in an area relevant to improving your key life sectors (sectors like finances, relationships, vocation, health and fitness, spirituality, and the like) and achieving your *WHY*. These criteria exclude mastering the facts involved in your favorite television series, memorizing statistics from your hometown football team, or being the most informed person in your workplace concerning the tragedy of world events. While increased knowledge in these areas would, by definition, improve your intelligence, it is not what we are aspiring for within the context of this aspect.

Baggage, Unclaimed, and Relevant Intelligence

To support this aspect's example, consider Fred, Frank, and Frances's decisions throughout their furlough during the COVID-19 pandemic as described in chapter four, which illustrate three primary types of intelligence.

BAGGAGE INTELLIGENCE

Fred *decided* to focus on and obsess over the aspects of his life he could not control: the ever-changing government mandates, news of the daily infection rate, and death count tallies. This enhanced knowledge created a form of intellectual baggage that burdened and distracted him from what would have been productive.

UNCLAIMED INTELLIGENCE

Frank *decided* to use some downtime to read a book on goal setting but could not keep his eyes off his nearby computer, where he was continually distracted by newsbreaks of business closures, soaring unemployment figures, updated government mandates, and stock market fluctuations. Recall that this unwillingness to make a choice to put the distractions away and focus on reading resulted in him never progressing past chapter one. The knowledge he missed out on, which remains unclaimed within those pages, could have changed his life.

RELEVANT INTELLIGENCE

Frances *decided* to invest her downtime by taking an online sales mastery course, reading one self-help book per month, and researching her competitor's products online. Each of the knowledge objectives sought by Frances during her downtime will impact, and are relevant to, aspects of her *WHY*.

BIG Bullet: To buy back time for more consistently acquiring relevant intelligence you may need to add some items to your "stop doing" list. Improvement is not always about doing more things, but in doing certain things less.

BIG Questions: To achieve your *WHY*, in which life arenas must you become more intentional in seeking knowledge? Are there areas where you have invested too much time acquiring baggage intelligence? What distractions must you eliminate or time must you schedule so that you can avoid futile efforts resulting in unclaimed intelligence?

2. I PRACTICE OR IMPROVE SKILLS.

This aspect refers to skills you already have: cooking, home repairs, writing, in your vocation, athletics, and more. It may also relate to skills such as listening, speaking, giving feedback, training, composing communications, and budgeting. A skill is defined as something you do particularly well or an ability to do something well; so, when evaluating this aspect, you are going to prioritize strengths you are making stronger. As a secondary priority, shift your focus to abilities you have that are not yet at skill level, and work to upgrade them to skill level.

Contrary to the cliché, practice does not make perfect and gives no guarantee you will improve. However, perfect practice will make a difference. Think about it: If you decide to work on your golf swing and double the number of balls you hit in practice but do it with the same flawed swing, you will only reinforce the defects in your abilities. First you must practice with precision and fix the swing. This applies to anything you are trying to improve through practice.

BIG Bullet: "I fear not the man who has practiced ten thousand kicks once, but I fear the man who has practiced one kick ten thousand times."[40] —Bruce Lee

BIG Questions: Which abilities important to reaching your *WHY* do you have that are not at "skill" level yet? How often do you intentionally work to improve them? What could you do more of, or do better? Where have you become so highly skilled that you may take the skill for granted and no longer work to improve it? How can you leverage your current momentum in those areas?

3. I ASK FOR FEEDBACK.

Bill Gates observed, "We all need people who will give us feedback. That's how we improve."[41] Unfortunately, many people have neither the humility, killer instinct, nor mental toughness to seek out feedback. In fact, when they receive feedback their ABLE reacts with the grace of a two-year-old tasting his first pickle, reflexively dismissing or arguing with the input and demonstrating a stronger commitment to the status quo than to changing their performance status.

Do You Want to Be Coached?

It is common and easy to declare a desire to grow and to ask for help to get better. But do you really want the feedback and coaching that comes with growth? Can you handle the truth? Are you willing to subordinate your feelings to your future? The answers say much about your killer instinct, mental toughness, and character. Fred, Frank, and Frances's different responses to feedback illustrate key differences in how most people respond. Which best describes you?

Fred hears feedback and pouts or agrees with it to get the giver off his back, but he changes nothing because of it.

Frank receives feedback and gets defensive, makes an excuse, or attacks the giver. He rarely even considers it and usually takes it personally. The only time Frank will ask for feedback is when he is fishing for compliments—the times he feels unappreciated or unacclaimed.

Frances seeks out feedback and acts on what she hears. She does not necessarily enjoy hearing the message, like how it is delivered, or agree with all of it, but she sifts through the dirt to find the gold. If it will help her improve and reach her *WHY*, she is willing to set aside her comfort zone and ego and give it a fair hearing.

BIG Bullet: Asking for and acting on feedback, rather than dodging, dreading, or dismissing it, reflects graduate-level coachability.

BIG Questions: How often do you ask for feedback on how you can improve? What is your first reaction when it is not what you want to hear? How likely are you to adjust to feedback that may help you but that you do not want to hear?

4. I ACT ON FEEDBACK.

If someone with a unique insight, greater experience, or notable success gives you suggestions or critique through feedback, you do not have to like or agree with it to act on it. In fact, the willingness to act regardless, in pursuit of the greater good of improvement, demonstrates maturity and hunger for growth. But if you are going to act on feedback, do the following four things:

- Act on feedback with the intent to make it work, not to prove someone else wrong.
- Do it with good ABLE, not as though you are two minutes into serving a thirty-year sentence.

- Invest your complete effort. Do not just go through the motions or do it for the sake of scratching it off your list.
- Understand that results may take time, so stick with it long enough to satisfy your conscience that you gave it your all.

When your *WHY* is strong enough you will follow these four points because you will prioritize personal improvement over the personal pride that has possibly inhibited your progress for too long.

BIG Bullet: Oftentimes nothing changes until you change something, and that something often results from feedback.

BIG Questions: Evaluate how you did in executing the four points listed with the last feedback you decided to act on. Which aspect of the four, if any, have you historically struggled with in the past and must improve?

5. I EXECUTE MY ACTION PLAN.

This aspect embodies the second half of intelligence's definition—"*applying* knowledge and skills"[42] —and refers to your success in executing your priorities before, during, and after work. If you know but don't do what you know, the next thing to know is that you must do better! This aspect is similar to, and somewhat overlaps, the discipline aspects of executing vital routines and commitments, as well as effort's aspect of executing your most vital tasks. Again, this pervasive emphasis throughout the ACCREDITED traits on giving complete focus and effort to what matters most *daily*, and limiting or eliminating altogether that which is unproductive, must become a resounding characteristic of your personal brand identity in all your life arenas.

Build Your Brand Daily

In the second aspect of the previous chapter I mentioned that keeping your commitments regardless of how you feel helps build your personal brand identity. When most people think of brands, they think of organizations, not individuals. But just like organizations, individuals also have a brand: something they are known for based on the experiences they create for other people. Fred has built a brand of being likable but underperforming; Frank's brand is higher performing and high potential but somewhat selfish and inconsistent; Frances's brand is thought of as relentless and consistent, as well as a bit aloof. If you completed the virtue section of the *WHY* workbook, you essentially defined what you would like your brand to be: You listed the traits that most define the person you wish to become, or to become more like. It is important that you complete that exercise, and here is why:

- **Once you more clearly define your personal brand identity, you have a benchmark for behavior to which you will hold yourself accountable.** If you want to become a "better person" or create "great performance," you must first define what those things mean to you.
- **Once your personal brand is defined, you are then more likely to choose daily behaviors that align with that identity.** This will influence you to improve your discipline and intelligence traits as you consider that every action you take in accordance with your ideal brand is a "yes" vote for the type of person you wish to become. Conversely, every time you act in a contrary manner to your aspired brand, including the inability to daily execute your action plan's priorities, you vote "no" for a better you. As with other elections, winning by unanimous decision is not necessary, but you will need to consistently earn more yes votes than no votes, day in and day out, to proceed successfully on the path to your *WHY.*

As will become very clear when you go through the ACCREDITED course, successfully executing and then grading daily the recurring themes like this one that you see throughout the ten traits will have either an unequally positive or negative influence on your daily scores. The reason for this is obvious in that the success or failure in the daily execution of those aspects has a disproportionate impact on your killer instinct and mental toughness, in you achieving your *WHY*, and on your life overall.

BIG Bullet: Great brands are built over time, not overnight. They are reinforced with multiple right and excellent actions, not one-hit-wonder bursts of adrenaline done excellently a single time.

BIG Questions: Is there a certain life sector you consistently fall short in when trying to do what you know you should do, be it financial, marital, parental, physical, vocational, spiritual, or other? Knowing that those deficiencies will not fix themselves, what can you do to become more intentionally intelligent and accountable for excellence and consistency in that area or those areas?

6. I TRY NEW THINGS.

Trying something new is uncomfortable, which is why it is so essential to growth. Even in small ways, trying something new can shake up a set mind, disrupt your comfort zone or a stale routine, or change your basis. *Sticking* with something new that is productive but perhaps uncomfortable should also be considered positively when grading this aspect during the ACCREDITED course. Even trying something new once, like food or drink, indicates a healthy openness to change.

New Things May Include . . .

- trying new foods or drinks
- making a new recipe
- doing anything that changes your basis in your routines: mindset, workplace, health/exercise, and the like. For instance, doing more of something productive you are already doing is trying something new. Even though the activity is the same, your effort to do more of it has changed. The same applies for doing less of something unproductive.

- daily writing in a journal
- reading a book
- listening to a podcast
- trying a new restaurant
- beginning a garden
- planting a different vegetable in your garden
- starting a weekly family meeting
- writing out a family mission statement
- taking a new online course
- watching an educational television program rather than a new sitcom
- trying a new hairstyle
- enrolling in a self-defense course
- taking a different route to somewhere you go often
- running your shower ice cold for the first ten seconds to jolt yourself out of a comfort zone early in the day

Even though some of these actions may seem to have nothing to do with "improving performance" per se, they nonetheless create a degree of discomfort and uncertainty that can positively influence and open your mind to changes in areas more directly connected to performance, and they should be factored in positively when evaluating this aspect.

Don't Cross the Line

There are, however, areas of your life where it is unwise and even destructive to try something new or "test the waters." These areas primarily represent, but are not limited to, actions that can be described as follows: vices or behaviors that violate your character and values, or that contradict the virtue-identity you are striving to achieve.

The world has many things you do not want to expose yourself to or experiment with in the slightest just because it is popular or because you are bored or in a rut. These actions can, over time, have a catastrophic impact on who you are trying to become, what you are trying to accomplish, and the impact you are aspiring to make.

Remember the Second Half

I'd be remiss if I did not nudge you here on the second half of intelligence's definition: you know, the "application" part. You must focus on consistent application in the productive new things you engage in and not just discard them because they were uncomfortable, difficult, unpopular, or did not bring instant results. You may recall from earlier in the book that killer instinct gets you started, but mental toughness helps you finish. You must adhere with what is new and productive and see it through to results. Remember how Frank decided to try a motivational podcast to fill his downtime upon Frances's recommendation? He found that continuing to listen to them rejuvenated and motivated him much more than his news and social media surfing ever did.

This aspect is not about trying vending machine sushi, getting sick as a result, and continuing to eat it daily to see if you have developed immunity. It is about sticking with the most relevant new actions you take rather than merely dabbling here and there and deceiving yourself into believing you are making progress. Try as you may, you cannot trick or manipulate growth in mental toughness in that manner. You must earn it over time.

BIG Bullet: "Only those who will risk going too far can possibly find out how far one can go."[43] —T. S. Eliot

BIG Questions: When is the last time you tried something for the first time? What something new have you delayed trying but will now reconsider?

7. I LEARN FROM MISTAKES.

Thomas Watson, founder of IBM, challenged his people to try more that is new with this quote: "If you want to increase your success rate, double your failure rate."[44] His rationale was that if one did indeed learn from mistakes and applied those lessons, one would become more successful because of it. We can turn the cost of our mistakes into bargains when we grow because of them and convert what we learned from them into results. Just as mistakes you fail to learn from will cost you again repeatedly throughout your life, so will the lessons we learn pay us time and again throughout the decades. And a generous return on that tuition paid to learn from a mistake is significantly escalated when we can share those lessons with others, and they improve too.

When evaluating your success in this aspect, you must also consider mistakes you repeated that day as a strike against your score, regardless of whether you learned from the initial error or not. Here is why: Sometimes you may learn a lesson from a mistake, but still fail to act in accordance with what you learned, thus demonstrating a deficit in the *application* aspect of intelligence. We should also remember that in cases of repeated mistakes, where lessons were learned but not applied, stupidity is evident and—if left unchecked—can unhappily become part of our personal brand.

IT TAKES TWO

If there were ever an area of life where "it takes two" is true, it would be in applying both aspects of intelligence: *acquiring* and *applying* skills and knowledge. You must not only apply what you know works or what has worked in the past, but must also leave your comfort zone, continue to learn better and more relevant things, and also apply those. The consistent application of what is no longer optimal is not going to get you to your *WHY* any more than becoming a walking, talking library of knowledge and skills that are rarely applied will. You must want your *WHY* ferociously to the degree that you learn and apply what is most relevant consistently enough to take you there. Salvador Dali put it well: "Intelligence without ambition is a bird without wings."[45]

BIG Bullet: Life does not reward knowledge, skills, experience, or talent. You must use those things to do something: something that is meaningful and consistent, executed with excellence.

BIG Questions: When it comes to intelligence, do you become lazier in your learning or in the application of what you learned? Why do you think that is the case? How can you remedy it?

INTENTIONAL ACTION

Consider areas of your life where your growth suffers most from the gap between knowing what to do and actually doing it: finances (budgeting or saving), health and exercise, building relationships, spiritual disciplines, the workplace, your downtime, overcoming vices, and the like. List at least three, then write a time-based step (start with just one) you will take to close that gap with meaningful action.

BADGERS ADVERSITY INCIDENT #11

January 28, 2020: Badgers Player and Team Leader Suspended One Game Resulting from a Controversial Call by the Officials in the Iowa Game

Already down the key player who quit the team, and reeling from blowing a late lead at Iowa, the Badgers needed new momentum to reverse their fortunes with time running out in January.

Brad Davison was the team leader, and for the next game the team would be without him due to a suspension following the Iowa game. Now down two key men, the Badgers would have to find a way to win against Michigan State, who beat them handily the last time they faced off.

PLAY A POOR HAND WELL

- How do you respond when you feel life is unfair, that you have been cheated, or that you just cannot catch a break?
- What do you do to shift your focus from what you cannot control to the next right step to take?
- How can you control your emotions and prevent unfair treatment from making you feel bitter or resentful?

Chapter Twelve

TENACITY

Hone a Rock-Hardheadedness

Tenacity is defined as "the quality or fact of being very determined."[46] The *very nature* of tenacity involves taking persistence to a relentless level. (Because of this I had playfully considered making this chapter incredibly boring and the longest in the book, so you would have to develop more tenacity just to labor through it!)

Before we get ahead of ourselves discussing the useful aspects of tenacity, let me disclose how this "rock-hardheadedness" can be potentially devastating: when you possess unhelpful hardheadedness—a determination to *not* change even when it is necessary, "pledging allegiance" to your comfort zone despite compelling and ongoing evidence that it is preventing you from fulfilling your *WHY.*

When I speak of *honing* a rock-hardheadedness, please note that "hone" means to sharpen or perfect. Thus, you can expect that the level of your tenacity's sharpness—knowing when to persist and when to change your methods or course—will be in direct proportion to the sharpness of your *WHY.* The clearer you get about what you want and why you want it, the more prone you are to adhere to the disciplines and principles that will take you there and avoid or discard what will not.

BIG Bullet: "If one advances confidently in the direction of his dreams, and endeavors to live the life which he has imagined, he will meet with a success unexpected in common hours."[47] —Henry David Thoreau

SEVEN KEY ASPECTS OF TENACITY

1. I STAY ON TRACK DESPITE OBSTACLES.

In the sixth and seventh aspects of discipline in chapter ten, I discussed how you must first define what the "track" is and that, while you will get off track from time to time, progress and growth require getting off track less often and recovering faster when you veer.

It takes tenacity to stay on track despite the many daily obstacles, distractions, and emergencies of the moment—some expected, but many for which you are unable to plan. When evaluating this trait, do not count how many times you got off track against you (that is best covered by the trait discipline), but by your hardheadedness in continuing to return to the priority at hand, regardless of what it may be: a conversation with your children, lifting weights, composing an effective email, executing your morning mindset routine, or completing an essential task at work. Every time you get back on track you build mental toughness, confidence, and resolve. And while it is easy to feel defeated when the setbacks persist, you are not beaten until you decide it is easier to stay on the wrong track than return to the right track that is difficult.

BIG Bullet: "When life knocks you down, try to land on your back. Because if you can look up, you can get up. Let your reason get you back up."[48] —Les Brown

BIG Questions: What can you do to eliminate or minimize the known distractions you can control? How can you become more mentally intentional in advance to return to a priority after you have strayed?

2. I PERSIST THROUGH TASKS WITH EXCELLENCE DESPITE DISTRACTIONS.

While the prior aspect concerned executing the right things despite disruptions, this point focuses on doing those tasks with excellence. This includes working to find ways to continually improve how you do them in your quest to compete with your former self.

Oftentimes when you have a setback, or are pressed for time as a deadline looms, you are prone to execute a priority casually or incompletely. You can know it needs to be done but lose sight of the fact you must do more than *do it*; you must do it very well. For instance:

- You do not just conduct an important meeting so you can say you held it, but instead plan it for maximum engagement and action.
- You would not carry out a coaching conversation with a teammate or employee and prioritize having a pleasant conversation over an effective conversation (sometimes they are two different things).
- At the gym you would not rush through five sets just so you can carry your sloppiness to the next weight station, but would rather work every repetition in perfect form.
- You do not hastily and carelessly fire off an email with unorganized thoughts, ramblings, and grammatical errors; instead, your emails are proofed and are composed with the intent to say more with an economy of words.
- You do not rush through a conversation with your teenager so you can check your text messages, but rather fully engage and listen more than you speak.

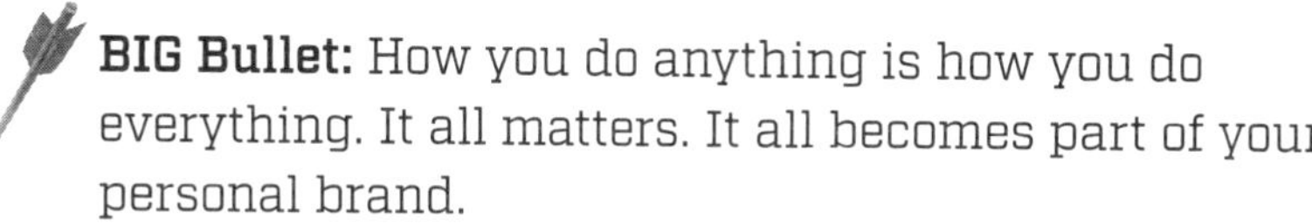

BIG Bullet: How you do anything is how you do everything. It all matters. It all becomes part of your personal brand.

BIG Questions: Which of your daily priorities are prone to suffer most from sloppiness or haste on the days your tenacity is worn down by distractions from many directions and bad news, or when you are multitasking through numerous duties? How can you become more tenacious at these times to double down on discipline so you can execute to completion with both excellence and consistency?

3. I KEEP GOING WHEN I FEEL LIKE QUITTING.

This aspect is to be evaluated in the context of completing priorities, not in bingeing on sitcoms or second trips through buffet lines.

Many people fail to develop tenacity because their goals are too small. If the bar is low, you can withdraw the struggle, discomfort, obstacles, disappointments, and uncertainty that influences the development of tenacity, killer instinct, and mental toughness. In this manner a low bar of expectations becomes a high barrier to improved performance. Consider the penalties of not expecting enough from yourself or others:

- There is little need to learn anything new since you can hit the goal with what you already know.
- There is no motivation to change anything since low goals can be obtained by doing business as usual. (The same goes for eliminating the need to risk, stretch, or make difficult decisions—all of which influence your growth.)
- You do not develop tenacity because low goals do not create potential pitfalls that cause you to have to fight hard, stick with it for long, get knocked off track, get back up after being knocked down, or figure out a better way.
- Focus, discipline, and consistency are not as necessary to reach easy goals, so your proficiency in those assets plateaus or declines.
- You miss out on opportunities to extend yourself, change your basis, and build the self-esteem and self-confidence required for bigger risks or larger goals.
- Hitting easy goals makes you think you are better than you really are.

- Low expectations give no incentive to improve over your former self, since your current self is already successful in achieving the little that has been prescribed.
- You have no real need for rigorous routines, including building your mindset and planning your day, since you are able to hit low goals void of those disciplines.

BIG Bullet: Low expectations for yourself presumes mediocrity within yourself. And when you presume mediocrity, you begin to create it.

BIG Questions: In which areas of your life have your goals become too certain, "slam dunks," or no-brainers? Which goals must you raise or broaden to evoke more tenacity and create the conditions for more discomfort and fight?

4. I MAKE MYSELF DO SOMETHING WHEN I DON'T FEEL LIKE IT.

Frank's Situational Tenacity

Frank is very determined to put in smarter and harder work, to plan his day, control his attitude, maximize his time, follow key processes, and go the extra mile . . . when he is behind his goal, struggling financially, or embarrassed because someone like Fred is getting close to beating him on the sales board. He also ramps up tenacity when he is closing in on a bonus or within reach of surpassing Frances's sales numbers. In these times when the situation is momentarily right for him, Frank will make himself do things he ordinarily does not do, nor particularly cares to do, even though he knows they are always the best things to do. Frank, like hordes of successful people in all fields, got good at what he does but never became great because being good provided him the option to turn on his tenacity only occasionally and still outshine most peers.

Frank's situational tenacity is what frustrates his manager, Alex, the most, for he sees what Frank is capable of when he is tenacious, but knows he lacks the killer instinct and mental toughness to make tenacity part of his everyday makeup. It is also what makes management appreciate Frances more: She does the right things regardless of how she feels and despite the fact she is number one because her *WHY* will not give her the option to do less.

BIG Bullet: The biggest determinant between being tenacious or not is the strength, or lack thereof, of your reasons for being tenacious—your *WHY*.

Chances to intentionally build tenacity by successfully executing the aspect of making yourself do something when you do not feel like doing it abound. Peruse this sampling and look for personal opportunities to improve this ACCREDITED trait today:

- make the apology you have been putting off
- return to writing the book you set aside
- send the rejected book you gave up on to ten more publishers
- say no to that cheesecake the next time everyone says yes (you will feel much better five minutes afterward than they do)
- stop saying "yes" to dating the person you don't feel is best for you because you are concerned about hurting their feelings or worried about being alone
- stop putting it off and go make your required number of calls today, then keep calling

- if you missed your workout this morning because you did not feel like it, do it tonight regardless of how you feel
- get out of your comfort zone and change your basis in at least three areas
- tell the truth to the person you have been avoiding
- hold that person accountable, even if they are your friend (especially if they are your friend)
- do not turn on the television tonight; instead, start reading the book you bought six months ago that has become credenza-ware

It is fair to say that none of this may be easy, but all of this will be worth it!

BIG Bullet: Mark Twain famously observed, "It's not the size of the dog in the fight, it's the size of the fight in the dog" that counts.[49] *That* embodies tenacity.

BIG Questions: Do you see a connection between the boldness of your *WHY* and the strength of your tenacity? What, if anything, can you do to make your *WHY* even more compelling so that failing to remain tenacious in its pursuit every day is never a part of your inner dialogue?

5. I REFUSE TO TAKE "NO" FOR AN ANSWER WHEN PURSUING A GOAL.

When developing and evaluating this aspect, keep this in mind: "No" is different than a distraction, emergency, or other obstacle. "No," in the context of this point, has a greater sense of finality or rejection to it:

- you did not get the job or were laid off
- you failed to make the team, or were cut from the team
- you did not lose a single pound in two weeks; you gained four
- someone you cared about dumped you

- your best sales prospect bought elsewhere
- the loan officer turned down your application
- your dream date never gave you a chance and rejected you
- you were mentally or physically exhausted beyond where you thought you could continue
- you flunked the exam
- you failed your martial arts promotion test
- you bombed your driving test
- the business you started must file bankruptcy
- the doctor gave you one year to live
- six colleges said they do not want you
- the business strategy failed, and it was your idea
- no friends you asked helped you
- your family disowned you

When "no" stands between you and your goals, and further progress toward your ambitions seems particularly dire, mentally regroup, learn from it, and take another shot with the goal of creating a more successful outcome this time. Don't let no become never.

BIG Bullet: When mentally tough people hit walls, they don't splatter; they bounce.

For Everything There Is a Season

Does the above heading apply to quitting or giving up? Actually, it does. In cases where you are in a toxic or abusive relationship, you are stuck in a company with no chance of advancement or that violates your values, you have worn the strategy out and it is still not working, or invested countless hours into someone who still will not change to help themselves, you must consider that it may be time to move on.

However, the goal of building an intentional mindset is so that you do not quit on the things or people in which you still see possibilities or that are essential to achieving your *WHY.* You do not abandon these endeavors just because it got tough, is taking too long, or because you are discouraged, really screwed up, or are not good enough yet. In fact, those are the precise times you must persist and remain very determined, for they offer unmatched opportunities to grow personally, earn self-confidence, cultivate humility, build character, sharpen focus, strengthen discipline, forge new habits, take personal responsibility, and accelerate your killer instinct and mental toughness to "Frances" levels.

BIG Bullet: Quitting because it is hard is easier than fighting through what is hard, but what is harder is *becoming* a quitter, living as one, dying as one, and having "quitter" as your legacy.

BIG Questions: What has historically been the most common "no" in your life that causes you to give up on a goal: the degree of difficulty, the time it took, rejection, lack of support, not being ready or good enough, having deficient self-confidence, not having the resources or connections, and the like? In retrospect, what is one productive step you could have or should have taken to this "no" that you can learn from and use to refine your tenacity going forward?

6. I AM UNFAZED BY CRITICS OR REJECTION.

In our own corporate offices in Agoura Hills, California, we have a plaque you pass before entering our facility with the word "UNFAZED" engraved on it. We were inspired to adopt that slogan one November as wildfires raged in our area, coming within one mile of destroying our offices, and knocking out internet and phone service for two weeks. During those challenges and distractions, our team rallied together, doubled down on what we could control, and, against crazy odds, made that same month the highest-revenue month of our year.

Unfazed means to be undaunted, unflinching, and not dismayed or disconcerted. If you want to become and remain tenacious, you must also become and remain unfazed, despite the hardships, critics, or rejection you endure along the way.

"Unfazed" is a mantra I had introduced to the Wisconsin Badgers men's basketball team in the 2018–2019 season (one season prior to that which is highlighted in the Play a Poor Hand Well sections), the day before they were scheduled to play conference rival Michigan. In the same meeting I taught the Red Belt Mindset concept to the team and gave a symbolic red belt to each player, along with the *WHY* workbook and a copy of my book *Unstoppable* (Wiley, 2017), and challenged them to clarify what they were fighting for not only in basketball but in life.

The Badgers had been struggling and were under fire from critics within both their fanbase and the media. The team would need an unfazed mental toughness as they prepared for their game the next day, January 19, 2019, on their home court in Madison against Michigan, who was ranked number two in the nation, losing only once in their prior thirty-two games, with a season win–loss record of 17–0. Rumors of the Badgers' demise were found to be premature, for when the Michigan Wolverines departed Wisconsin that afternoon, they were 17–1, suffering a shocking ten-point loss at the hands of an unfazed team of mentally tough Badger Red Belts.

BIG Bullet: When others say you are history, turn their tale into fiction.

Without an intentional mindset, critics can own and control your attitude, enthusiasm, focus, passion, and more. They can drain you, create self-doubt, shatter your daily routine, train-wreck your tenacity, and plant within you seeds of stress, resentment, or bitterness. Some critics even become haters, resorting to personal attacks that have nothing to do with performance, spreading rumors or gossip, labeling you, and not just disparaging your results but demeaning your humanity. Sometimes critics are strangers, those you do not know or have heard of but never met. They are on social media and in the workplace, and many reside within one's own family. If you surrender your mindset to critics, they will pitch their tent of terror within your head and live there rent free; they will control you, own you, and beat you down without ever physically engaging you. Following are six thoughts to build a healthier perspective on critics:

- Not all critics are the same. You can learn from reasonable critics and critique. Thus, you should not summarily dismiss all critics or criticism. With the right mindset you can use critics and their observations or ideas to improve.
- Some, no matter what you do, you will never please. You have got to learn to be okay with that.
- What they say or think does not define you unless you let it.
- Debating or engaging them, especially on social media, empowers them and lets them control your time and impact your emotions.
- Develop an affirmation that becomes part of what you read each morning during your mindset routine to build a powerful mindset against them. I have two affirmations with wide application that have worked particularly well for me concerning critics: "They don't matter" and "I choose cheer." When I am unfairly criticized or attacked by haters, those two thoughts, ingrained into my thinking over many years of intentionally wiring those affirmations into my mindset, remind me to keep perspective.
- Critics are often envious, attacking those who are what they would like to become or who do what they would like to do. They do not necessarily hate you; they hate themselves for not being like you, doing what you do, or having what you have.

Rejections, rebuffs, or being turned down, left out, or left behind do not define you either—regardless of whether they concern your ideas, efforts, affections, or attempts at reconciliation. If rejection causes you pain, use that pain to steel your focus, broaden your *WHY*, deepen your resolve, strengthen your mental toughness, and sharpen your killer instinct as you regroup to try again. Everyone suffers through rejection. What will make you stand apart is how you choose to let it affect you: as something that happens to you or for you; to be a victim or to move closer to victory. Pout momentarily if you must, but then inventory the lessons or opportunities; grow stronger, wiser, and better than before; and take another shot.

BIG Bullet: "I don't care what you think about me. I don't think about you at all."[50] —Coco Chanel

BIG Questions: What typically causes you to become fazed and lose your focus and tenacity? Can you create a personal affirmation that wires your mind in advance to become more impenetrable to those factors?

7. I HAVE ENCOURAGING SELF-TALK.

What do you say when you talk to yourself? Everyone talks to themselves. *What* they say to themselves, however, greatly influences either tenacity or surrender, confidence or compromise, drive or defeat. Often done unconsciously, disempowering self-talk is common and self-destructive:

- "I'll never figure this out." Better version: "I'm going to figure this out."
- "I'm going broke." Better version: "I'm learning lessons I will apply to work myself out of this mess."
- "I'm next to be fired." Better version: "I'll make myself so valuable they can't fire me."
- "I never get it right the first time." Better version: "I'm going to get it right this time."
- "I'm just not good enough." Better version: "I'm not where I want to be, but I'm not where I used to be either."
- "No one wants to be with me." Better version: "I have a lot to offer, and the right person will be worth the wait."
- "I'll never change." Better version: "I can change, and I will change."
- "I've never been good enough." Better version: "I'm committed to getting better."

Beware that unhealthy self-talk can also absolve you from responsibility, create a victim's mindset, or invite arrogance into your life. While some statements like these may have degrees of truth, they can still be unproductive and deplete killer instinct and mental toughness—they reek of self-pity and pride:

- "I never get enough credit."
- "It's not my fault."

- "I didn't have time to do it."
- "I deserve better than this."

BIG Bullet: The world throws enough negative voices your way without you lending your lungs to the beatdown.

BIG Questions: Do you have affirmations you use as part of your morning mindset routine to wire your mind in advance and power through adversity with tenacity? Which can you specifically create or add for that purpose?

TENACITY IS A CHOICE

How many goals have you missed, not because the goal was not worthy, but because you got distracted, tired, depressed, or decided to quit before reaching it?

How many have you achieved because you decided up front that quitting was not an option and powered through to reach it?

In either case, you made decisions that determined the outcome. Missing the goal was not just bad luck any more than reaching it was simply good luck. As was discussed in chapter four, "Decisions Determine Direction," when you feel stuck in the middle of a long and tough journey, you may not be able to see how or when you can possibly finish, but you don't have to know that much or see that far. All you need to see is how to get to the next step in front of you. And then choose to take that step. Then repeat.

BIG Bullet: "Let me tell you the secret that has led me to my goal. My strength lies solely in my tenacity."[51]
—Louis Pasteur

INTENTIONAL ACTION

What are at least three worthy endeavors you started but did not finish: a book, workout program, morning mindset discipline, rising at a certain time, diet, martial arts instruction, online course, college degree, and the like? Pick one that you regret most that still has possibilities and that you would like to start up again. Then decide when and how to do it. List the first step, then do it quickly.

BADGERS ADVERSITY INCIDENT #12

February 5, 2020: Minnesota Blows Out the Badgers by Eighteen Points

After a string of setbacks in January, the Badgers could start February strong with a win against their border-state rival Minnesota, setting the tone for a run through March.

Just prior to the game, news broke that beloved Badgers strength and conditioning coach Erik Helland, who had not traveled with the team to Minnesota, was under investigation concerning his offensive choice of words in a private conversation with four Badger players, where he related a Chicago Bulls player's pre-game mantra heard during his time on the Bulls coaching staff. The Badgers were soon after embarrassed by an eighteen-point loss in the typically tough border-state battle.

PLAY A POOR HAND WELL

- How can you tune out the world's news, noise, and buzz—especially when it is negative—to focus on the matter at hand?
- When the consequences faced by a loved one hang in the balance and are out of your control, or when that loved one is apparently being treated unfairly, how can you help that friend and others stay motivated and productive?
- How do you continue to bounce back from adversity when you are tired, or when the world and its events seem to conspire against you? How can you prevent a victim's mentality in such situations and use the adversity to your advantage?

Chapter Thirteen

ENERGY

Fuel a Fanatical Focus and Fight to the Finish

It is common to relate "energy" solely to physical activity. This assumption excludes energy's mental component. Energy is defined as "the strength and vitality required for sustained physical and *mental* activity."[52] While drive, covered in the next chapter, is entry-level killer instinct and instrumental in motivating you toward your goals, energy powers you to complete the journey. It provides the physical stamina to remain productive for the duration, and the mental fortitude to stay locked in and engaged so you can think clearly and execute well during the process. To that end, it is essential to become a more intentional daily manager of your physical and mental energy. This begins with your morning mindset routine and persists through the rituals, challenges, objectives, tasks, ups, downs, problems, and opportunities each day presents.

BIG Bullet: Drive without energy starts fast but fizzles. Energy without drive lacks the focus to invest itself wisely.

WHY, Water, and Level

Frank saw Fred coming his way and winced. He liked Fred but had learned that spending time with him was not normally productive.

"What's her secret?" Fred asked.

"Whose secret?"

"Frances's."

"How do you mean?"

"She never runs out of gas. Early, mid-day, late in the day, doesn't matter. The beginning or end of the month makes no difference either. She's always in motion."

This was the first time Frank could remember Fred talking about Frances in an almost admiring way, without taking a shot at her. "You know, I asked her that myself one time," Frank said, "and she credited three things: *WHY*, water, and Level."

A puzzled look came across Fred's face as clear as the salsa stain on his collar. "What? *WHY*, water, and Level? What the heck does that mean?" he questioned.

"Don't you remember in that meeting when management asked her to explain how she stays motivated and consistent, and she explained that her *WHY* was her goals, her reasons for doing what she does? She said she reviews it every morning before coming to work."

"I vaguely remember that, but I pretty much tuned her out because it sounded like a bunch of touchy-feely mumbo jumbo."

"Well, it must work for her. She even showed us that she keeps her *WHY* on her computer. It's pretty extensive; she's got it divided into five categories—"

"*That's* where she lost me," Fred interrupted. "It seemed extreme and over the top."

"Maybe, but it's hard to argue with her results."

"What's the big deal about water?"

"Hydration," Frank replied. "She said the first thing she does when she wakes up is drink thirty-two ounces of water."

"I drink coffee."

"She does too, but after she drinks the water."

Fred challenged, "Well, why all that water?"

"She told me she'd read that everyone wakes up dehydrated, which is why you feel sluggish early on. So, drinking water first thing in the morning replaces what you lost while sleeping. I took her advice, and it works. I feel alert faster. I do need to drink more during the day, though. She drinks something like a bottle an hour."

"All I need is a couple of Red Bulls and I'm golden. Well, what's the 'Level' thing about, then?"

"It's a high-grade nutrition bar she buys online as a snack, or sometimes a meal. She gave me some, and they're great. Oat cookie is my favorite."

"That's nuts! You're telling me her *WHY* and more water make her a sales freak? Come on, there's got to be more to it than that."

"Don't forget the nutrition bar. You know, Fred, those burritos, Red Bulls, and doughnuts you graze on all day aren't helping you. What you eat influences how you feel. I mean, you wouldn't put low-grade gas in a Ferrari, would you?"

"No, but—"

"So, you can't put garbage into your gut all day and expect to be sharp. Besides, if she says those are the keys, I believe her. And give her credit . . . if she's a 'freak,' she's a freak by design. She does this stuff every day and I still haven't beat her on the sales board," Frank said.

"Whatever. All sounds far-fetched to me. Talking about food made me hungry, though. I'm going to grab a Moon Pie. You need anything?" Fred asked.

"I need to beat Frances this month. Get me a bottled water, please."

BIG Bullet: Building and sustaining higher levels of energy is not about doing extraordinary things, but doing the ordinary things extraordinarily well. Again and again.

As with so many aspects of the ACCREDITED traits, working to improve an area of your life is often as much about what you don't do as what you do, and intentionality plays a major role in executing the good and avoiding the unproductive. Without enough energy, killer instinct can go flat, and mental toughness can fall short. Increase your energy, however, and you fuel and sustain greater killer instinct and mental toughness in all your vital life sectors.

SEVEN KEY ASPECTS OF ENERGY

1. I INCREASE MY MENTAL STRENGTH BY BUILDING AND GUARDING MY MIND THROUGHOUT THE DAY.

Building and guarding what goes into your mind each day is a recurring theme because how and what you think determines whether you do what is most effective, how well and often you do it, and whether you do it despite a lack of feeling like doing it. On the days you engage in an effective morning mindset routine and reinforce and strengthen your thinking throughout the day, you will score well here.

BIG Bullet: A healthy mindset is never done or set. It is like a garden, requiring constant weeding, seeding, and watering, lest it be overrun by the weeds, diseases, bugs, and outside elements bent on its destruction.

BIG Questions: Do you feel a difference in mental energy, motivation, and focus on the days you invest in your mind early in the day and avoid media immersion? If your mindset routine stops energizing you or challenging you, do you tweak it and raise your basis to keep it optimally relevant and effective?

2. I DON'T ENGAGE IN EVENING ACTIVITIES THAT DRAIN MY ENERGY TOMORROW.

It is common to speak of getting up on the wrong side of the bed, but that act is actually initiated when you go to sleep on the wrong side of the bed in the first place: getting too little sleep or poor-quality sleep; late-night snacking or excessive alcohol intake; evening arguments or pre-sleep social media debates. The last thing you should do before going to bed is watch or read the news and subject your subconscious to a garbage buffet while you are supposed to be resting. Sleep is not just about resting your body but your mind as well, and the higher-quality your sleep, the less sleep you require.

Ending your day well can be as simple as:

- filling out your gratitude journal in the evening and listing all that went well that day
- developing a discipline where both you and your significant other share three things each that you appreciate about one another
- exercising
- engaging in spiritual disciplines
- listening to or reading something inspirational
- fasting from food the final few hours before retiring
- making certain you are well hydrated before you sleep, since sleeping dehydrates you

BIG Bullet: Ending well precedes starting strong.

BIG Questions: Are you intentional enough when it comes to ending your day well? What could you do, or should you stop doing, to improve this vital discipline for managing energy productively?

3. I HAVE HIGH LEVELS OF ENERGY AND ENGAGEMENT IN ALL MY LIFE ARENAS.

You are more likely to do well with this aspect if you are motivated by a *WHY* that includes goals in all life's arenas: health and fitness, family, friends, workplace, hobbies, spirituality, personal growth, and the like. Also, as you begin to improve your execution of strategies like those in chapter nine on effort (working harder smarter and smarter harder so that you are not resigned to putting in unnecessary additional time at work as compensation for time you misused), you will have more time to fully and energetically engage in these aspects. This is another example of how the ten ACCREDITED traits can either positively or negatively impact the others, based on your progress and consistency in developing each to higher levels.

BIG Bullet: One-dimensional excellence or achievement eventually feels shallow, empty, and unfulfilling.

BIG Questions: In which area of your life must you improve performance by doing more of what matters, so that energy is less wasted and more preserved for investing intelligently into your other vital life sectors? What will you do specifically to accomplish that? Determine the same for your other essential life sectors as well.

4. I STAY MENTALLY LOCKED INTO THE TASKS THAT MATTER MOST.

This discipline applies to wherever you are in the moment: workplace, conversing with a friend, writing a paper, in the gym, listening to a spouse, reading a book, attending a class, and the like. Working to master this aspect in *any* of your vital life sectors maximizes your use of mental and physical energy in *all* of them.

BIG Bullet: Little improvement tweaks of rightly applied energy, invested across multiple life sectors, evoke an exponential return on one's total performance. Little letups in the same measures evoke a compounding return of detriment and fatigue.

Working to master the art of full mental engagement, to truly *be there*, wherever *there* happens to be, is as rewarding results-wise as it is personally fulfilling. You simply feel more alive when you are engaged mentally, as well as physically, in what you are doing at the moment. This leaves less room for stress, worry, or other energy leaks that can make you feel worse about the day, the world, yourself, or your life. However, successfully pursuing this level of engagement has never been more challenging, as it competes with a rising and pervasive level of technology-driven distractions fired at you daily with relentless consistency—vying for your attention and energy 24-7.

BIG Bullet: Refusing the bait of distraction is a discipline.

BIG Questions: When are you most prone to be somewhere physically but someplace else mentally? What must you *stop* doing so you can engage your energy more fully into the task or life sector at hand? How will you increase awareness of the need to execute this action?

5. I POWER THROUGH WHEN PHYSICALLY TIRED WITHOUT "RESTING" AT WORK.

This aspect of energy ties in well to the principles outlined in chapter nine, "Effort: Work Harder Smarter and Smarter Harder." It is about disciplining yourself to consistently align your energy with the most essential tasks at the moment. There will always be times when you get physically and mentally tired at work. Get used to it. To grow and progress, use these times to change your basis, persist, and build mental toughness, living daily as a person powered by a *WHY* so compelling you can do nothing less.

BIG Bullet: To paraphrase the Second Law of Thermodynamics, things naturally wind down; they do not wind up unless outside energy is applied. Make certain that energy is applied in the areas of your life you want "winding up" and that you are not leaving unattended those things that must not wind down.

Put a Brake on Breaks

It was 9 AM, and all the sales team had clocked in and started their workday. Alex began his morning routine of checking in with each team member to go over their appointments for the day. Finishing up with Frank, he moved on to Fred's desk just as Fred was finishing up a doughnut and a Red Bull.

"Fred, are you on break already?" Alex asked. "It's only 9:15 AM."

"No, I usually take my break around ten. Why?"

"You just got here, you clocked in, which means we're paying you, and the first priority for your workday is eating?"

"I know I'm eating, but I'm hungry," Fred lamented. "I don't always have time for breakfast at home."

"Then get up earlier or get more organized so you can eat before you come here. The objective of being at work, Fred, is to work. You have two ten-minute breaks and a full hour for lunch. That's three chances to eat during your eight-hour shift. Either eat at home, or don't eat until your first break, but you're not going to get your job done coming to work with a priority of something other than work. Does that make sense?"

"I think you're making a big deal out of nothing, Alex. You're treating me like a child."

"No, I'm treating you like a professional, even though you're not acting like one when you don't work at work. One reason you have to work your days off to make your quota is that you don't invest your energy into the right things during your normal shift, and this is a prime example. Let me put it more clearly: Miss a meal if you have to, but don't miss your work priorities." Alex spun to leave, turned back, and said, "You know, Fred, you'll survive missing your daily doughnut if you have to, but you're not going to survive in this business if you keep missing your priorities."

Fred dabbed the jelly off his chin, took the second doughnut from his desk, wrapped it in a napkin, and shoved it in a drawer before going to greet an unassisted customer. He hoped the guy would not require a lot of time. He was not sure how fresh the napkin and drawer would keep the rest of his breakfast. Hopefully, it would still be good at 10 AM after his burrito. Chocolate iced doughnuts were his favorite, and he had saved it for last.

BIG Bullet: When you misdirect energy and irreplaceable time into what matters less, you can adjust and do better going forward. But you do not get a do-over to regain what is forever lost.

BIG Questions: How often do you misapply energy while at work so that you are not *working* at work? Can you grasp the accumulative devastation "two minutes here" and "five minutes there" have on your results over the course of a day, week, year, and career? Do you recognize how the same principle adversely impacts energy misspent in all your life sectors? How will you fix this?

6. I AVOID ENERGY LEAKS.

An energy leak, within the context of this aspect, is anything that gives you a less-than-optimal result on energy invested as relates to your *WHY*. Obviously, that covers a ton of ground, much of which we have discussed in previous chapters. Because there is vast opportunity for error concerning misapplied energy daily, there is an equal opportunity to improve as well. Here is an obvious but necessary sampling to build perspective on how wide-ranging energy leak traps are:

- news media obsessions or overloads
- mindless television, radio, and online games
- social media addictions or debates
- a critical spirit
- worry
- executing tasks you should delegate
- engaging in trivialities while priorities are left undone
- stewing with bitterness or anger
- trying to change people who do not want to change
- reading "trash" publications online, in print, or anywhere
- moral vices
- always trying to have the last word
- excessive sleeping in
- trivial, whiney, gossipy, speculative, or otherwise unproductive conversations (conversations held too long or too often with the "Freds" of your workplace)
- unhealthy or excessive food or drink
- judging others
- road rage
- trying to control whom or what cannot be controlled
- blame and excuses
- envy
- concern over what a peer is doing or getting
- pouting about something not going your way
- an egotistical commitment to always being right
- seeking vengeance or trying to get even
- manipulating others
- lying and dishonesty
- cleaning up messes resulting from being ill prepared

- doing again what you did not do right the first time
- revisiting the same issues with someone because expectations were unclear
- seeing it as your role to put everyone in their place
- not learning lessons and repeating the same mistakes
- failing to take notes, then having to ask again later what was said
- speculation over what could happen but is unlikely
- unforgiveness and resentment
- stress brought on by any or all of these

While this sampling is nowhere near complete, it offers an eye-popping picture of how easy it is to misspend energy and continue off track without an acute awareness to promote avoidance and faster recoveries.

BIG Bullet: Little leaks, left unchecked, become gaping holes of missed potential over a lifetime.

BIG Questions: Which energy leaks in your own life have gone on for too long and created detours on the path to your full potential? What will you do about it starting today?

7. I EAT ENERGIZING FOOD AND STAY HYDRATED.

Data, forums, journals, doctors, health experts, and best sellers espousing the connection between eating right and improving energy levels abound. We know what to eat, what to avoid, what improves energy, what offers only a temporary spike, and what essentially drains our energy from us. But as we discovered in the chapter on intelligence, *knowing* is only half the equation, and to be considered wholly intelligent we must also *do* what we know. Sadly, by that standard most folks' eating and drinking habits would relegate them as intellectual half-wits!

Comparatively, little attention is given to the importance of hydration. When evaluating and improving this aspect of energy, pay particular attention to this underrated, lethargy-busting daily discipline. And yes, hydration is a discipline, one that is easy to overlook but requires the same awareness as eating healthy.

BIG Bullet: Don't mistake the obvious as unimportant.

Dehydration is defined as "a harmful reduction in the amount of water in the body."[53] It results from a negative fluid balance: more going out than coming in. When your body is in this state you are affected both mentally and physically:

- **Dehydration thickens your blood, and thus your organs must work harder, consuming energy.** Hydration helps your organs work smarter, not harder.
- **Dehydration can raise blood pressure and cause headaches, irritability, short-term memory loss, anxiety, and fatigue.**[54] The more water you put in, the less these afflictions pile on.
- **Twenty percent of kidney stones are attributed to dehydration.**[55] Choose the "pain" of hydration discipline over the pain of regret.
- **According to a study of 3,003 randomly selected people, 75 percent were dehydrated.**[56] Based on this, staying consistently hydrated gives you a performance edge over most people you encounter.
- **Dehydration is the primary cause of midday fatigue.**[57] Hit the water bottle, not the Red Bull.
- **By the time you feel thirsty, you are already dehydrated. It requires only a 1 to 2 percent net fluid loss to cause thirst.**[58] Early and often beats late and lagging.
- **Flying on aircraft, where up to 50 percent of the very dry air is brought in from high altitudes, dehydrates you. What is often attributed to jet lag is, in fact, dehydration.** A few-hour time difference causes less jet lag than too little water.
- **Signs of dehydration: an inability to sweat, dry skin, bad breath, dark urine, and urinating less than six times per day.** The signs are obvious, but so is this particular solution.

- **It is possible to still be dehydrated after drinking a lot of water.** Caffeine, alcohol, and the contents of energy drinks can hamper your hydration discipline. Use them in moderation, and use water in excess.
- **Hydration can boost your metabolism.**[59] Cold water is especially effective in this regard since the body spends more energy heating up cold water.
- **Because of your net fluid loss while sleeping, you awaken dehydrated.** Drinking 16 to 30 ounces of water soon after waking can energize your mornings. Intaking caffeine without drinking water in the morning further dehydrates you and makes you lethargic. Thus, the lament of many people that "I'm not a morning person" may be attributed to their dehydrated state. If your morning breath is renowned for its ability to knock a buzzard off a dung wagon, keep bottled water at your bedside and down it as soon as your feet hit the floor. (This could improve the relationship aspect of your life as well.)

BIG Bullet: "You changed my life by getting me *more* hydrated on flights! I'm coachable; I listen!" —From NBA skills trainer and friend Phil Beckner, after practicing my recommended discipline of drinking 12 ounces of water per one hour of airplane flight time

INTENTIONAL ENERGY

At this point, it will not surprise you that developing an intentional mindset, and consistently and purposefully practicing simple eating and drinking disciplines, can have a profound impact on your moment-by-moment energy levels. Build energy, replenish it, and manage it well, and your daily journey is not only more fruitful in results, but you just plain feel better in the moment as you increase your alertness, stamina, focus, and physical well-being—all of which are supporting cast components of developing mental toughness and a killer instinct.

BIG Questions: Does your daily diet generally energize you or drain your energy? How conscious are you of staying hydrated throughout the day, right up until the time you go to bed? What do you normally drink as your morning drink, and does it hydrate or dehydrate you?

INTENTIONAL ACTION

When it comes to building, replenishing, and managing your daily energy levels, decide in which life arenas your current habits or tendencies are your own biggest foes. Try to find at least three, and create a simple and workable action step to address your self-afflictions.

BADGERS ADVERSITY INCIDENT #13

February 5, 2020: Losing Streak of Four out of the Last Six Games

The blowout loss to rival Minnesota cumulated a downward spiral of another devastating losing streak and at the worst possible time. The season had only a few weeks remaining.

Pressure had been mounting on the players and coaches for weeks to get it together and finish the year strong. Losing the last four out of six games this late in the season strengthened the argument of critics that this year's season was a lost cause.

PLAY A POOR HAND WELL

- When time is running out to reach your goals, and others doubt or criticize you, how do you keep from doubting yourself?
- How do you stop only showing up physically and going through the motions while quitting mentally and emotionally?
- After being battered for the duration, how can you find one last-second wind to finish well?
- Do you have a mindset to convert the misery you endure to create memories you will one day cherish?

Chapter Fourteen

DRIVE

Become a Driven Driver, Not a Driver Who's Driven

You have nearly done it! You are close to completing the final ACCREDITED trait chapter and, before long, moving on to the seventy-day course. Drive helped get you here, and you will need it to finish this book and the subsequent course as well. So, let's keep moving!

A "driven driver" is one whose motivation comes from within and powers them to drive toward their *WHY* daily. On the other hand, a "driver who's driven" is one who must be prodded, cajoled, bribed, threatened, or otherwise motivated by outside forces. It should come as no surprise at this point that the primary differentiator between the two is the power of their reasons—their *WHY*.

Drive can be considered baseline killer instinct. While drive prompts you to attack opportunities, especially those that come your way, killer instinct motivates you to seek out or make those opportunities. But rarely does one move from a passive status straight to killer instinct, in a sustainable manner, in one fell swoop. Drive is a first and necessary progression toward that end.

Following are seven aspects of drive that require evaluation and improvement to firm your motivational foundation and position you for the higher levels of growth in killer instinct and mental toughness you will need to achieve your *WHY*.

SEVEN KEY ASPECTS OF DRIVE

1. I DO A QUALITY JOB REVIEWING MY WHY.

If you review your *WHY* during your morning mindset routine, you may have noticed there are days you are rote, rushed, distracted, or preoccupied during the process. When this occurs, you are missing the impact that comes with visualizing each element of your *WHY* and strengthening the emotional connection that takes you from merely reading the goal to seeing and feeling it. It is the seeing and feeling of it, more than skimming it, that heats up your drive.

BIG Bullet: Moving your *WHY* from head to heart is a must—a catalyst for making drive and energy combust.

Fred Figures It Out

Fred was waiting at Frank's desk. "Where've you been?" Fred asked.

"I was in the men's room. Would you like a report?" Frank snapped. "Drinking this extra water not only hydrates, it keeps you in motion. I need to get a desk closer to the toilet."

"I still don't buy the hydration hype, Frank, but I want to know more about the *WHY* thing. Do you have yours in writing? I may want to use it as a basis for mine. I'm thinking about writing it out and reading it in the morning to get me going."

"It doesn't matter what mine is about, Fred," Frank replied. "Your *WHY* is personal. It needs to relate to you. There's not a wrong one or right one. Make it about you and your life."

Fred answered in his polished and practiced victim's voice, "But I don't even know where to start."

"Look, Fred, you should do what I did and go talk to Frances. She's the resident expert. She even went to a website and downloaded a workbook that explains the *WHY* and walks you through it."

"I don't think Frances likes talking to me much."

"That's not true, Freddy boy. I've seen her try to help you a lot, and it looks more like you don't like talking to her."

"It's a little embarrassing to get help from a woman, especially since I've been here longer than she has," Fred admitted.

"What ought to embarrass you, Fred, is opening your mouth and having foolish sounds like what you just said fall out of it. You've been here longer but your results aren't getting any better. Swallow your pride and go ask if she has time to explain more about it. That's what I did. Now, I've got an appointment coming in five minutes, so I need to get ready."

Fred watched Frank hurry off. He was getting tired of being talked down to. He might not be the best performer on the team, but he was not the worst either. *If only these guys could have seen me back when I was the high school football star*, he thought, *they'd be more respectful*. He dreaded asking someone like Frances for help. In his view, with all she had going on in her life there's no way she should outperform him: single mom, special-needs kid, recovering alcoholic, pain-in-the-butt ex-husband. But his job, or rather his life overall, was missing something. He knew it. His wife knew it. Everyone knew it! Maybe the *WHY* thing would help. It sure couldn't hurt. He was tired of drifting through life getting the scraps and leftovers. He was not getting any younger either. Fred saw Frances coming back from lunch and headed her way, resolving to skip his traditional Monday munchies at McDonalds today to spend time on his *WHY* if he had to. It was time to get some help.

BIG Bullet: If you don't take the first step, you can't take the second.

BIG Questions: If your drive level is too inconsistent in any life sector (getting healthy; in the workplace; as a spouse, parent, or friend; and so on), which aspects of your *WHY* need to be amended or added to give you more reasons to be a driven driver? What aspect of your WHY could you broaden or embolden so that you are more motivated and less stagnant?

2. I CHOOSE AND REVIEW MY LANDING PLACE.

Drive is diminished when you get off track during the day. Your landing place is your guard against getting off track, or staying off track for too long, during the day. It is your couple of key priorities for that day that give you a place to come back to if you deviate off course. Hopefully, at this point in the book, after seeing this aspect recur in various forms, you are executing it daily. You simply *must* have something meaningful to attack and channel your drive toward, and your daily landing place (your handful of key priorities) provides the target.

BIG Bullet: Well-directed drive creates consistency and facilitates fulfillment.

BIG Questions: Have you started identifying, scheduling, and reviewing the highest-return activities daily? Are you staying ready, or do you continually have to *get* ready because you became mentally unready?

3. I DON'T REQUIRE EXTERNAL MOTIVATION.

Waiting for pats on the back, pep talks, additional financial incentives, or other forms of motivational rescue to get you going is a sign you still have some serious inner work to do. You cannot control whether you get external motivation, so if you are dependent on it you are turning the motivational keys of your life over to people and things beyond your control, which is a recipe for personal powerlessness.

Without question, it is nice to be noticed, complimented, rewarded, applauded, or affirmed; it is *nice*, but it should not be *necessary* for you to feel motivated or driven. Here are eleven key points concerning your drive level:

Your Drive Is Your Job

- Your drive must start from within by building a more intentional and focused mindset.
- Your drive must be intentionally fed and sustained from within.
- When your drive wanes, you can, and must, recover it quickly.
- It is your responsibility to avoid people and activities that drain your drive.
- Your drive is ignited when you have a *WHY* worth fighting for.
- Your drive is sustained when you resolve to compete with your former self daily.
- Your drive must be managed well daily and directed into what, and who, matters most.
- Your drive should be quickened by external motivation, not ignited by it.
- When you do not get credit you think you deserve, power on to make an impact that is impossible to ignore.
- Requiring excessive amounts of motivational rescue marks you as a high-maintenance team member.
- Work to mentally liberate yourself from the prison of depending on another's approval to feel good about yourself or your performance.

BIG Bullet: You should not require external motivation to get going. You should already be going! External motivation should simply get you going faster.

BIG Questions: Is your attitude or performance ever negatively impacted by an absence of external motivation? How can you make another's external affirmation matter less in your life?

4. I FOCUS ENOUGH ON THE GOALS THAT MATTER MOST.

"Bad" activities do not normally get in the way of goals that matter most as often as the "good" and "great" ones do. With a more intentional mindset and stronger killer instinct we have the sense to avoid altogether, or at least to limit, the time spent focusing on bad things: the actions or thoughts that are entirely unproductive and sometimes destructive. Normally, it is the good and great things that compete with the handful of best things that matter most. It requires significant discipline and mental intentionality to set aside or subordinate what is good or great to pursue relentlessly the goals that matter most—the best things. This is not to say you should not focus on or work toward your lesser goals, but rather that you prioritize time and resources into what is *best* before you address those that are subordinate.

For instance, if your goal (or goals) that matters most looks something like one of the examples below, evaluate whether you are giving it the focus and drive it deserves, or if you need to redirect focus and drive from less essential areas.

- getting a job
- becoming debt free
- buying a new car, house, and so on
- saving for your child's education
- earning an A in a course
- writing a book
- leasing a new jet
- losing twenty-five pounds
- making the team
- building an orphanage
- securing the promotion
- mastering a second language
- successfully completing an educational course
- endowing a university

- ridding yourself of toxic anger or bitterness
- passing your next rank in the martial arts
- balancing your budget
- launching a new business
- reading the Bible from cover to cover
- developing a consistently excellent morning mindset routine
- starting your own podcast
- being elected to political office
- making it through rehab
- quitting an addiction
- saving your marriage
- selling your invention

BIG Bullet: Misapplied focus squanders drive and sentences best goals to death by neglect.

BIG Questions: Are there major goals supporting your *WHY* that you need to redirect misplaced drive and focus toward each day? What must you temporarily give up so you can more measurably go up?

5. I FOCUS ENOUGH ON WHAT I CAN CONTROL.

You may wish to review the sample list of areas in your life you can control, mentioned back in chapter five. As life's crises and critics rage around you, it is easy to lose focus on these powerful possibilities for daily progress. Giving time, energy, conversation, and focus to aspects of life you cannot control dampens your drive because feelings of helplessness and powerlessness ensue.

BIG Bullet: Good luck working for what you want most while whining about what you can affect least.

BIG Questions: Which "uncontrollables" do you still focus on too frequently: weather, economy, competition, coworkers' behaviors, media stories, tabloid gossip, trying to change people who do not want to change, critics and haters, and so on? How can you make these factors less worthy of your time and attention?

6. I FEEL UNSTOPPABLE DESPITE CONDITIONS.

In chapter four we discussed the importance of making right decisions to marginalize tough conditions. When evaluating this aspect, did tough conditions cause you to:

- take a shortcut?
- give up?
- complain, make an excuse, or enroll in the blame game?
- lose emotional control?
- allow your ABLE to become disabled?

If factors like these affect your trajectory for long or too often, you cannot consider your performance as being unstoppable. On the other hand, if you rose to the challenge and powered on, remained unfazed, followed prescribed processes, and executed your priorities with excellence despite adverse conditions, you will have earned high marks with this aspect.

BIG Bullet: When the going gets tough, the tough don't have to "get going" because they never stopped going in the first place.

BIG Questions: Do unexpected challenges bring out the best in you, or the distress in you? When everyone else hits the panic button, are you the one who remains calm and steady, or are you more prone to join the chorus of chaos? Can you see how developing more confidence and resilience feeds an unstoppable mindset?

7. I AVOID UNDRIVEN PEOPLE AND DRIVE-DRAINING ACTIVITIES.

I have written at length about unproductive actions, so I will focus here on the dangers of closely or often associating with undriven people in your workplace, circle of friends, and the like. This is not to say an undriven person is a bad or wrong person, but that their thinking is a bad and wrong fit for anyone wanting to develop their killer instinct and become more mentally tough. Undriven people may consciously, or unconsciously, influence you in the following ways:

- They can make you feel guilty for working hard because it makes them uncomfortable.
- They can mock your rigorous routines because they make them uncomfortable.
- They can point out your weaknesses or flaws to help "bring you down to size" or otherwise make you feel worse about yourself—which makes them feel better about themselves.
- They can fill your head with the pollution of their excuses, blame, or other nonsense that wastes your time and inflicts an unproductive influence on your thinking.
- They are inclined to talk negatively about other people to take the focus off their own performances or lives.
- Their poor habits in speech and actions can influence and rub off on you.

BIG Bullet: "Show me your friends and I'll show you your future."[60] —Mark Ambrose

BIG Questions: Inventory the people you spend most of your time with and the activities you engage in most often. Put them in one of two categories:

- ignites or fuels my drive when I engage with them
- douses or distracts my drive when I engage with them

Which list is longest? And is that okay?

Bonding over Bourbon

"Hey, Frances, you want to go to Mel's with Frank and me?" Fred asked. "We're stopping in for a little celebration before heading home. We need to toast our record month!"

It had been over a year since anyone on the team had asked Frances to a get-together after work. And Fred? *What got into him?* she thought. Maybe the time she spent helping him with the *WHY* principles the past few weeks had softened his opinion of her. She did not want to go, but somehow felt she should. "Well, you guys know I can't have the hard stuff, but as I recall Mel makes a pretty good virgin piña colada. I'm in."

Frank chimed in, "Chris might join us too. I told him a few of us might go there and invited him."

"I like Chris. I hope he shows," added Fred. Chris was one of two team members who consistently performed worse than Fred. Fred liked not being the bottom guy in the group.

"Try not to overdo it, guys," Alex cautioned. "We had a great month, but tomorrow we start all over again. I need you all mentally checked in and ready to go."

"No worries, Alex," Frank said sarcastically. "We're limiting it to two and Frances is basically having a pineapple milk-shake. Consider it a quick bonding over bourbon session. We'll be fine."

Deep down, Alex was pumped to see a few of the team going out to enjoy their success together, especially this odd mix: the top gun, the perennial runner-up, the lovable loser, and Chris—he wasn't sure Chris was going to make it with the company.

"There he is!" yelled Fred as Chris walked into Mel's. "Just in time too. As soon as I finish this one, I'm out of here."

"Sorry I'm late, guys, and I can't stay long," apologized Chris. "Just between us, I have a phone interview for a job tonight and I want to be sharp. I just stopped in to let you guys know what's going on. I might be leaving the company."

Chris's abruptness caught Frank off guard. "You're quitting us?" Frank asked.

"Well, I want to have a job lined up first, but yes. I'm pretty much finished. I just don't think Alex likes me, and everyone says I picked a rough time of the year to get into this business. The economy is making it tough to be in commission sales right now, too, so I need to find something with a more stable paycheck."

"Chris, you shouldn't give up on yourself this fast," Fred said. "Every reason you just mentioned for not selling more is out of your control, and you can't focus on that stuff. There's plenty more you can do to be productive every day. I'm sure Frank and Frances would help you figure that out. And I'll do whatever I can too. Believe me, I've learned a lot about what not to do the past couple of years. You don't want to be a quitter, Chris. You need a *WHY* worth fighting for." With that, Fred picked up the apple crisp Level bar Frances had given him. "Fourteen grams of protein and adaptogen superfoods, right, Frances? Never thought I'd give up pork rinds and beef jerky in a bar, but this is actually pretty darned good. I'm going online and getting some."

As Chris hurried off and Fred reveled in the bite of bar with a final sip of bourbon, Frank and Frances exchanged shocked looks.

Fred stood up. "See you guys tomorrow. How much do I owe you for my part?"

"I've got you covered, Fred," Frank said, still stifling a chuckle after listening to Fred give his tough-love pep talk to Chris. "See you tomorrow."

"Appreciate it, Frank."

As Fred walked out the door, Frances asked in disbelief, "What . . . just . . . happened?"

Frank laughed. "Maybe our friend Fred is growing up a bit and figuring things out, Frances. He did have his best results ever this month. He could get on a roll. And if *he* can change, it ought to give Chris hope."

"I hope you're right, Frank. When Fred was giving his 'Lombardi speech' to Chris, I couldn't believe what I was hearing. I was afraid Mel accidentally spiked my drink with rum and that I hit my head falling off the wagon!"

Frank laughed. "No, you heard right. I couldn't believe it either. Hearing Fred, of all people, say those things inspires me to step up, too." Frank paused, then laughed again, "Did I really just say that out loud? Let's get out of here. I want to get packed tonight. After work tomorrow we're going to visit my dad for the weekend."

Frances was cautious. "How are you and he getting along these days?"

"Better. I think I'm starting to understand him more. I'm through trying to compete with him. I just want to go there and be a good son."

"Good for you, Frank. I know how much he used to stress you out. Let's go. I promised Amy we'd build a fort tonight in the living room."

"How's she doing, Frances? Haven't seen her since the Christmas party."

"She's the most positive kid and has such a beautiful spirit. There were two new boys on the block who made fun of her last week during our walk. She cried for like twenty seconds, then was back to being happy Amy."

"Some punk kids made fun of her? Because of her disability? Where do they live?"

Frances laughed. "They're nine years old, Frank; don't beat them up just yet. See you tomorrow."

"Take care, Frances. And Frances, next month is *the* month."

"What do you mean *the* month?" Frances asked.

"The month I beat you in sales and end your streak."

Frances laughed. "Bourbon makes you brave, Frank! Be sure to give it your best shot so when I beat you again, we'll both know it was when you were at your peak."

"Fair enough," Frank shot back. "A little friendly competition will make us both better." As Frank walked to his car, he knew he would need to raise his game to back up his words.

Driving home, Frances thought about how Frank still didn't get it. He was treating her like she was his competition. But in reality, he was still his own worst enemy and until he learned to get out of his own way, she would keep beating him. Especially since she would approach the upcoming month like she always did: to compete with her own performance from the prior month. And since that month happened to be her personal best, she had her work cut out for her—competing with her best former self and not Frank's best efforts.

BIG Bullet: "He who cannot establish dominion over himself will have no dominion over others."[61] —Leonardo da Vinci

BIG Questions: Who or what dampens your drive and enthusiasm and is more likely to stifle you than inspire you? What will you to do limit or eliminate your association with these factors?

INTENTIONAL ACTION

Are there drive-draining activities or people you need to limit your time with or avoid altogether? List them. Then decide on a substitute activity to put in their place. Remember that even trading in ten minutes per day of drive-drainers for something more productive compounds substantially over a lifetime.

BADGERS ADVERSITY INCIDENT #14

February 6, 2020: Coach Helland Resigns

After losing four of the past six games, the Badgers were grasping for any inkling of momentum they could find to help them reverse their course and finish the season strong.

After being given the option to resign or be terminated, Coach Erik Helland opted to resign after seven years as the Badgers' strength and conditioning coach, taking responsibility for his actions and exiting with class. The team had now lost key players and staff during the second half of the season, just when they needed to excel to have a shot at making the NCAA tournament.

PLAY A POOR HAND WELL

- What do you do when consistent hardship makes you feel "enough is enough": Do you quit, or dig in and fight harder?
- What aspects of your character are revealed in adversity? How can you catch yourself faster when you fall into the "blame game" and get back to what is productive? How can you use adversity to shape your *WHY* and make it more compelling than before?
- When all seems lost, do you have a strategy for stepping back, gaining perspective, regaining focus and resolve, and finding your second wind?

Chapter Fifteen

THE ART OF PLAYING A POOR HAND WELL

At the conclusion of each of the past fourteen chapters I shared an Adversity Incident from the Wisconsin Badgers men's basketball 2019–2020 season. The goal in each instance of the Play a Poor Hand Well sections was to help you consider how you would handle similar situations in your own endeavors, applying strategies you have learned or refined from reading through this book. While the context in this chronology was basketball, the challenges were universally relatable:

- staying focused, positive, and productive amid setbacks, distractions, disappointments, or defeats
- recovering from setbacks, distractions, disappointments, and defeats
- honing killer instinct and strengthening mental toughness as you progress through life's challenges
- finding a way to win when the odds are against you
- remaining positive and productive despite critics, haters, and detractors
- using killer instinct and mental toughness to overcome talent gaps
- using what appears to happen *to* you *for* you by finding a way to use it to your advantage

- converting injustice, betrayal, loss, and doubters into compelling components of your *WHY*
- fighting on even when shorthanded, under-resourced, or facing long odds
- believing in yourself after others have quit you or stopped believing in you

For a fresh perspective, here is the chronological summary of the Badger Adversity Incidents reported in each chapter. I've added the insights of the Wisconsin Badgers Head Basketball Coach Greg Gard to share his thoughts on what was learned from the Adversity Incidents and how the team responded, benefited, and persevered.

1. **May 25, 2019:** Fatal automobile tragedy of Coach Howard Moore's family
Coach Gard: "These were undoubtedly the hardest and darkest days of my personal and professional career. There is no classroom, textbook, or video training that can prepare you to be ready for such a catastrophic chain of events. I could only revert back to an experience I had in 1995 while an assistant coach at UW–Platteville. We had a player (Gabe Miller) pass away after the season from a torn aorta that occurred during a flag football game. I distinctly remember those dark days and how our head coach, Bo Ryan, handled the ensuing adversity and grief experienced by all: You rally the troops—circle the wagons tighter than ever. No one else outside our team and family mattered. Literally, you walk day by day, sometimes it was hour by hour. There were many times when you didn't know what to say—and there are times that you best say nothing because you could never find the proper amount nor satisfying combination of words. In leadership—whether in games, a season, or real-life adversity—'when the waters are the roughest, it's imperative you be the calmest.'"

2. **June 24, 2019:** Coach Moore's heart attack
Coach Gard: "If you can go from bad to worse, this was Webster's textbook definition. As if the previous month hadn't been grueling enough, now I had to deliver a message on a late June afternoon to a group of young men who were already emotionally walking on thin ice. I had to be real. I had to be honest. Because if I wasn't, and painted a brighter picture than what was reality and something happened for the worse, I'd lose their trust. Our staff (both medical and coaching) tried to deliver as much information as we were allowed to the team . . . I'm not sure they all grasped the gravity of it, but we had to shoot straight. They saw raw emotion from our staff—up close, personal, extreme emotion—we leaned on each other. And I kept re-emphasizing—'we need to stay together and be there for one another.'"

3. **November 5, 2019:** Season opener overtime loss to St. Mary's
Coach Gard: "My response was not to overblow the situation—it's game one of a long season. It was a loss to a good and experienced team. This was our first game without Howard on the bench, and the pre-game ceremony was also the first time he, his family, and the chain of events had been publicly recognized in front of the team. It was going to be emotional—I knew that coming in—and it was. My message was that we're never as good or bad as we may appear to be at times, so learn from this game, get better, and move on—fast. W = Win and L = Learn."

4. **November 21, 2019:** Micah Potter eligibility waiver denied again
Coach Gard: "Micah was always the adult in the room. I never got overly optimistic about his reinstatement, and always expected and planned for the worst. He was getting robbed of his career and the only clock ticking was on him. I was upset and have often said that the 'Office of Common Sense' fails to exist at a lot of institutions in today's society. But we had to keep going—we couldn't sulk and make excuses about what or who we didn't have helping us. You can't lose what you never had, right? We had to get better with who

we did have on the floor and not drown ourselves in self-pity over who we didn't have."

5. **November 25–December 11, 2019:** Losing streak of four out of five games
Coach Gard: "I'll consolidate my thoughts on both our losing streaks [this and point thirteen] with this: We needed to get better—needed to shoot it better in certain stretches. I've never looked at streaks, whether good or bad. We were playing good teams, on the road, and if you don't play well, it's a recipe for disaster. But we always operated in a 'next day' mentality. Don't get paralysis by analysis—focus on what you can control and don't let what you can't control control you. Be the windshield, not the bug—be the hammer, not the nail—be the boxer, not the bag. Learn, get better, move on, prepare for 'next.' Have thick skin, control the 'controlables,' trust the process."

6. **January 8, 2020:** 71–70 home loss to Illinois after leading the game late
Coach Gard: "We lost to a good team that was gaining confidence. We held a late lead and then didn't execute well enough down the stretch. We had not practiced well the day before—and it showed in little things that night. I reminded the team of the previous day's practice—ownership and accountability weren't where they needed to be yet. Lesson learned—you will play how you practice. Get comfortable being uncomfortable. 'High achievers don't like to be around mediocre people and mediocre people don't like to be around high achievers.'"

7. **January 17, 2020:** 67–55 loss to Michigan State after two top-twenty-five wins
Coach Gard: "They were better than us that night. I reminded myself to 'not over-react and don't under-react' . . . Learn, get better, move on. Don't overanalyze it. Never let one loss beat you up so bad mentally that it causes you to not prepare for the next

challenge as soon as possible. We are bad as coaches, as we tend to agonize and put ourselves through misery after a loss ten times more than what we enjoy and take satisfaction in after a victory. The key was 'don't lose to Michigan State twice.' And we didn't."

8. **January 24, 2020:** Blowout 70–51 loss at Purdue
   Coach Gard: "We got blitzed early, didn't execute well offensively—didn't respond well mentally to not shooting it well. I made my points after the game and during the next day's film—we didn't compete hard enough. And we did what we often warn against—'Never tie your emotional state to your jump shot.' We needed to get tougher mentally—stop feeling sorry for ourselves. Soon we would figure it out and turn the corner. Get better—fast—and find a way to move the needle."

9. **January 26, 2020:** Second-leading scorer quits the team
   Coach Gard: "This actually unified the ranks of our team even more than I thought it would. It was really evident in our game at Iowa—even though we lost, we had great fight and resolve. We played hard—we competed with some guts and heart—in a time when we could have easily chosen to go 'belly up' and had all the excuses to go along with it. The character of the team had been revealed—I liked what I saw—we were going to be okay. I told them that night and the next day in the film study that our coaching staff would go to battle with that group of men that played last night—if that groups shows up, we'd be just fine. We played together, unified, and more for each other than for their individual mindset. Any 'energy vampire' needed to be changed or removed. Going forward, if we tried it any other way, which we had, we'd be just good enough to get beat."

10. **January 27, 2020:** Six-point loss to Iowa after leading by twelve points late in the game
    Coach Gard: "This may have been the galvanizing game that rocketed us to what would happen later. We fought, we battled,

we won thirty-five minutes—the problem is the game was forty minutes. We started to believe in ourselves completely. We didn't feel good about losing, but had comfort in how we competed and played inspired together. If we could duplicate this effort we'd be just fine. As the year evolved, we became less consumed with ourselves and learned not to care about anyone on the outside or what they thought or said. We figured out that the only ones who really matter were the teammates in the locker room with us. Basically, anyone on the outside was an enemy. We became completely consumed with playing for our team and being there for each other. Nothing and no one else mattered."

11. **January 28, 2020:** Team leader Brad Davison suspended one game
    Coach Gard: "Again, the team used this as a rallying cry. We grew to become less 'Brad dependent' for vocal leadership, resiliency, and toughness. Others found their voices. Sometimes the best way to get unknown leaders to step up is for the flames to get hotter and higher with no one to bail them out. Leaders can't be afraid of confrontation."

12. **February 5, 2020:** Coach Erik Helland rumors go viral; lost by eighteen points to rival Minnesota
    Coach Gard: "This was an expected but often unavoidable emotional dip from the previous win versus Michigan State as we rallied around the Davison suspension and beat them despite being without Brad. It was also the first game without Coach Helland. A lot was swirling around our guys—I could sense it. They needed our support—it had come to an absolute 'circle the wagons' time. This was going to be make or break for us—but because we had seen so much shit over the past seven to eight months, we had a different level of resolve, a different level of calloused-ness to us. It would serve us well going forward."

13. **February 5, 2020:** Team has lost four of the past six games
    Refer to point 5 for Coach Gard's comments.

14. **February 6, 2020:** Strength and conditioning coach Erik Helland resigns under fire
    Coach Gard: "I'll summarize the events of February 5th and 6th by saying it was controversial and emotional, but because we had been through so much and had seen so much adversity, what was another gut punch? We took it in stride, and again, rallied for each other. The only senior who was playing, Brevin Pritzl, did an excellent job of helping to fill the 'vocal void,' especially when it came to on-court functional movements. He stepped up and found his leadership niche at the absolute perfect time. We also had other staff members with our program (strength staff, trainer), including my coaching staff, step up big time. Everyone helped to raise our bar . . . all rallied, all succeeded."

BIG Bullet: "Every adversity, every failure, every heartache carries with it the seed of an equal or greater benefit."[62] —Napoleon Hill

As happens to us all as we progress through our life journey, each player and staff member on this team had their killer instinct and mental toughness tested time and again by circumstances and events often beyond their control. Guided by a key aspect of their collective *WHY* to honor Coach Moore, the staff and team found silver linings, applied lessons, and determined to take what appeared to happen *to* them and make it happen *for* them. In fact, this phrase became common locker room conversation as the season progressed. Head Coach Greg Gard, who came under intense criticism and endured demands for his firing throughout the year, including "Fire Gard" signs hung in student dormitories, did his best to keep his team together and never stopped believing in his players, the staff, their cause, or himself.

After the last Badger Adversity Incident listed on February 6, 2020, here is how the season's final month unfolded for the Wisconsin Badgers men's basketball team:

- **February 9, 2020:** Badgers defeat Ohio State 70–57
- **February 15, 2020:** Badgers defeat Nebraska 81–64

- **February 18, 2020:** Badgers defeat Purdue 69–65, avenging their earlier loss
- **February 23, 2020:** Badgers defeat Rutgers 79–71, avenging their earlier loss
- **February 27, 2020:** Badgers defeat Michigan at Michigan 81–74
- **March 1, 2020:** Badgers defeat Minnesota 71–69, avenging their earlier loss
- **March 4, 2020:** Badgers defeat Northwestern 63–48
- **March 7, 2020:** Badgers defeat Indiana at Indiana 60–56 in the season's final regular season game, after being behind by nine points in the second half
- **March 7, 2020:** Badgers finish the season as one of the hottest teams in the country, with eight consecutive victories to win the B1G Ten Conference Championship (Michigan State and Maryland would later earn a share of the title)
- **March 9, 2020:** Wisconsin Head Coach Greg Gard, target of the "Fire Gard" brigade, earns B1G Ten Coach of the Year Award from media and coaches and later named NABC District 7 Coach of the Year
- **March 9, 2020:** Badgers earn the number-one seed in the upcoming B1G Ten Conference Tournament
- **March 11, 2020:** B1G Ten Conference cancels tournament due to COVID-19 pandemic
- **March 12, 2020:** NCAA cancels the men's and women's basketball tournaments; season is over
- **March 13, 2020:** Badgers positioned to again play a poor hand well by applying lessons learned throughout the season to prepare for what's next

The Badgers, who had trouble much of the year finishing well to win games, closed out the season on a run that brought to life their season's motto and purpose to "Do Moore. Be Moore. 4 Moore." At the conclusion of the locker room celebration after defeating Indiana and winning the championship, an emotional Coach Gard gathered his staff and team of unfazed, Red Belt, B1G Ten champions around him and said, "Adversity . . . it obviously started back in May. That was more adversity . . . I felt if we could get through that, there was nothing we were going to see in the season that mattered. That was real-life adversity. And it's ironic," pausing as he moved to a whiteboard in the locker room, where he continued by writing on it the final score of the game that clinched the championship for them, in the form of an equation: 60 – 56 = 4 Moore.[63]

Gard said later, "There is no doubt we've had some help from above. How ironic that we won by 4 Moore. I can't wait to take this trophy back to Howard and let him touch it."[64]

BIG Bullet: When there's a *WHY* that's big enough, there's a way that's sure enough.

The one thing you can't take away from me is the way I choose to respond to what you do to me. The last of one's freedoms is to choose one's attitude in any given circumstance."[65]

—Viktor E. Frankl

Chapter Sixteen

THE ACCREDITED COURSE

Tailor Your Ten Weeks

If you have chosen to continue your journey to accelerate your mental toughness and killer instinct and take the ACCREDITED course, please consider the following thoughts on the process:

- You will spend one week developing and evaluating each of the ten ACCREDITED traits discussed in the book, focusing on the seven aspects of each trait.
- The Personal Progress Diary at the back of the book serves as your "scorecard" as you evaluate and improve each trait during your journey.
- You may join our free Insider Club at LearnToLead.com, where you will have access to the Diary in a downloadable form, as well as access to seventy corresponding and brief videos to support your journey (one video for each of the seven aspects within the ten traits).
- You are welcome to either start the course with a specific trait you wish to prioritize, or to go through the traits in the order presented.
- We recommend you review the seven aspects of the particular trait you will be focusing on during your morning mindset routine, and then proceed with your evaluation before retiring for the evening.

- To accelerate your progress and growth you may wish to go through the course multiple times and to focus more on certain traits the second or third time around.
- If you get off track and miss days, or drop out of the course altogether, get back on track! This, in itself, is a test of mental toughness.
- You may wish to work through the course with others who have also read the book so you can compare notes and hold one another accountable.

BIG Bullet: Simply starting the ACCREDITED course is a test of killer instinct. Your ability to finish it with excellence will change your basis and gauge your mental toughness.

PRESTON POWERS ON

You may benefit from the real experiences a team of leaders shared as they went through the course following a seminar I taught them. A client for many years, the Preston team has had major success. Their hunger to continue to grow and improve despite their success is inspiring. As you learn of their ups and downs throughout taking the ACCREDITED course, you should gain guidance and encouragement as you prepare to take your own journey.

I am including some background information on the group so you may understand more about their makeup and their leader, Dave Wilson. While Dave defines an entrepreneurial spirit and is involved in many ventures, the highlights are as follows.

Dave Wilson started in the automotive business in 1977 selling cars at Preston Ford and became a partner in 1981. At the age of twenty-two he was Ford's youngest first-generation dealer. Dave now owns fourteen automotive dealerships. In February 2019, he was inducted into Ford's Top Volume Hall of Fame. Preston has gained national recognition for its massive success since the town of Preston, Maryland, has a population of only 700 people! In 2019, Dave's original dealership, Preston Ford, ended the year ranking thirty-third in sales out of more than three thousand Ford dealerships in America. All fourteen dealerships have been recognized by their manufacturers for high customer satisfaction and high sales efficiency. In 2015 Dave founded iFrog Marketing Solutions. Dave chairs Provident State Bank and Triton Automotive Group, a dealer-owned product and services group. In Dave Wilson's own words, he chronicles his and his team's experience with the ACCREDITED course:

> Going through Dave's ACCREDITED course was a real learning experience for me. I was at a two-day leadership seminar when Dave Anderson first introduced the idea of his ACCREDITED course and the seventy-day course challenge. Leaving that seminar, I had accepted the challenge and fully intended on completing the course. Eagerly, I started the very next day and diligently plugged along for the first two weeks. Then I got lazy and complacent, and just couldn't manage to stay focused. I got off track and stayed off track.
>
> Five months later, as we attended a follow-up seminar in the same setting, Dave asked us how we all did with the course. A few of the leaders raised their hands when asked who had completed the course. I looked around and saw lots of people not making eye contact with Dave. I raised my hand and asked Dave if I could ask some questions.
>
> I asked my group how many started the course. About half of the people out of the sixty-five in the room raised their hands. I was one of them. Then, I asked how many finished the course. Only a few hands remained. It really hit me hard and was something that took time for me to wrap my head around. I know our group is very disciplined and we strongly believe in Dave's leadership training, so I asked myself, "What went wrong?"
>
> I always say the speed of the leader is the speed of the pack. I took a long, hard look in the mirror and realized I had performed poorly, and so had our team. In fact, I couldn't get my mind off of my poor performance. I asked who would want to go through this challenge with me again. Who would want to hold each other accountable? I had a few people commit right then at the meeting.
>
> When I arrived home after Dave's seminar, I wasn't happy with the amount of people who wanted to take the seventy-day challenge with

me. Rather than wallow in self-pity, I took action. I sent a compelling and genuine email to our leadership group. Ultimately, more people decided to take the journey with me.

Over the next few days, we sent out a binder with the Personal Progress Diary and reiterated the need to hold each other accountable. Fourteen of us, roughly 20 percent, started the ACCREDITED course together. We set up a text group to keep everyone engaged. We were all committed to help each other complete the ACCREDITED course and conquer this seventy-day challenge to build more mental toughness and killer instinct.

As soon as we got going, COVID-19 hit, and it hit hard. It really affected every single one of us. States were closing businesses. As everyone knows, businesses were being designated "essential" and "non-essential." We were deemed to be an essential business. Even with all this flux, the one thing that didn't change was this group continued to stay on track with the seventy-day challenge. We pushed each other. We checked on each other. We made sure everyone was continuing to stay true to their commitment to work through the course. It would have been very easy to use COVID-19 as an excuse for falling off track again. Instead, this team became more committed and united. For myself, I stayed more focused on what mattered most. The safety and well-being of our associates at all of our companies was my priority. The timing of coming back through this challenge and the unwavering commitment to finish was a godsend to me and my fellow leaders. We even started sharing motivational videos, quotes, and Scriptures.

We called each other out if one of us didn't respond to a text. It was truly amazing. We were holding one another accountable. Week after week, this group got stronger and more committed. We stayed dedicated in the hardest of times.

Personally, I started working out harder. I had gotten off track from my workout routine early in the year, and watching Dave's videos struck something inside me to get back to my old self. I vowed to get back at it, and I did. I spent more time with Dave's *Game Changer Life* podcasts, and also more time in his online virtual training university.

As we neared completion of the seventy days, I found myself wishing we had more days and weeks left.

I was mentally and emotionally back; locked in. So, what did I do? I sent out another message challenging our entire leadership team to join me in repeating the challenge again. Guess what?! Seventy percent of the original group raised their hands again and another five leaders not in the original group joined. It was amazing. COVID-19 was still in full force; we all knew this would help us be better leaders, and it was as if we needed to stay united. We needed to continue holding one another accountable. This group was even more engaged the second time around. We pushed each other hard. The new members were just as charged up. Text messages were going off early in the morning and late at night.

I decided to do something different this second time through. I was having trouble with defining and reviewing my *WHY* and reviewing my daily landing place. I did two courses and scorings a week: going through the traits and curriculum in order, while simultaneously grading my drive every week. That's ten weeks of DRIVE. It helped me a ton and got me laser-focused on my *WHY* and landing place while revisiting the other nine topics. I turned into an animal and watched my fellow associates do the same. No one got off track because we wouldn't let each other. We found ourselves even checking in on the phone with each other. Making sure everyone was okay during the pandemic and never letting each other get off track was our mission. We completed the next weeks, and as the world seemed to be moving so slowly in all other aspects, our seventy-day journey seemed to be moving so fast. As we were coming down the homestretch a second time, I got the idea to ask if anyone wanted to go through the ACCREDITED course again a third time.

Wow, was I surprised: We had twenty-four leaders raise their hands. As of this writing, we are all in week two. This group is relentless and laser focused not only on the course, but also in maximizing results during COVID-19.

Personally, I am firing on all eight cylinders in all aspects of my life and business. My daily routine has never been better. My relationship

> with my family and coworkers is rock solid. I find myself checking in on several people daily. I have always considered myself disciplined with a tough mental mindset. The ACCREDITED course got me back on track daily and gave me the tools to empower other leaders.
>
> The funny part is, each time we got to the trait of tenacity, I received text messages outside of our group saying you should be scoring high on this section. I looked at my scores and I wasn't scoring myself high. I pushed harder each day in this section to live up to our team's expectations of me.
>
> Unlike other courses I have taken, I stay engaged with the ACCREDITED seventy-day challenge. My goal is to be able to continue to grade myself with a "5" in the sixth aspect of drive, feeling unstoppable despite conditions, with the help of this challenge!

As you may have ascertained from Dave's experience, while taking the course individually will be an incredible growth experience for you, including others with you on your journey will elevate both your and their results to an entirely different level.

IT'S UP TO YOU

As is true with so much of your life that determines your future, what you do from here is your choice:

- Retool your *WHY*, or make the rest of your life up as you go along.
- Realign your daily priorities, or major in minor things.
- Subscribe and listen to *The Game Changer Life* podcast for reinforcement and support, or begin a new Netflix series.
- Visit the Insider Club at LearnToLead.com and begin watching the seventy ACCREDITED videos and download extra Personal Progress Diaries, or post more photos on Facebook.
- Drink more water, or buy more Red Bull.
- Visit LevelFoods.com for a healthy snack, or shop MoonPie.com.

- Join a gym, or your third fantasy football league.
- Start the ACCREDITED course today, tomorrow, next week, or never.

There is nothing I can say at this point to further stress the mandate for an intentional mindset to build more mental toughness and a stronger killer instinct that I haven't said repeatedly throughout these pages. You can be a Fred, Frank, or Frances; the boxer or the bag; the Red Belt in the arena or the critic on the sideline; the Level bar or the Moon Pie. My hope for you is that you will continue the journey and stretch yourself, improve your mindset, raise your basis, narrow your focus, subordinate your feelings to your future, and add both years to your life and life to your years.

BIG Bullet: "We should every night call ourselves to an account. What infirmity have I mastered today? What passions opposed? What temptation resisted? What virtue acquired? Our vices will abort of themselves if they be brought every day to the shrift."[66] —Lucius Annaeus Seneca

BIG Questions: Of the options listed, which will you make next, and what impact will they have on your future and the lives of those you love most?

THE ACCREDITED COURSE PERSONAL PROGRESS DIARY

ATTITUDE

A settled way of thinking reflected in one's behavior.

Evaluate your attitude based on the following scale

1 Strongly Disagree → 5 Strongly Agree

DAY:	1	2	3	4	5	6	7
I responded well to negative things.							
I was not easily offended.							
I demonstrated positive speech.							
I focused on what I could control.							
I was able to maintain grace under stress.							
I avoided blame and excuses.							
My words and actions made others feel better about themselves.							

OBSERVATIONS & REFLECTIONS

COMPETITIVENESS

Striving to gain or win something by defeating or establishing superiority over others who are trying to do the same. (The primary "over others" is your former self).

Evaluate your competitiveness based on the following scale

1 Strongly Disagree → 5 Strongly Agree

DAY:	1	2	3	4	5	6	7
My attitude was superior to yesterday's.							
My habits were superior to yesterday's.							
My focus was superior to yesterday's.							
My discipline was superior to yesterday's.							
My knowledge was superior to yesterday's.							
My drive/energy/motivation was superior to yesterday's.							
My results were superior to yesterday's.							

OBSERVATIONS & REFLECTIONS

CHARACTER

Evaluate your character based on the following scale

1 Strongly Disagree → 5 Strongly Agree

A combination of moral and ethical qualities that determine the individual nature of a person.

DAY:	1	2	3	4	5	6	7
I was honest in words and deeds.							
I was accepting of responsibility.							
I kept my commitments.							
I gave complete effort at work.							
I put others first.							
I controlled my tongue.							
I remained humble and teachable.							

OBSERVATIONS & REFLECTIONS

RIGOR

The quality of being extremely thorough, exhaustive, or accurate.

Evaluate your rigor based on the following scale

1 Strongly Disagree → 5 Strongly Agree

DAY:	1	2	3	4	5	6	7
I scheduled my priorities in advance.							
I was successful in executing my priorities.							
My daily routine was more effective than yesterday's.							
I made productive use of downtime and commute.							
I budgeted time to improve.							
I made time to add value to others.							
I focused more on key activities than outcomes.							

OBSERVATIONS & REFLECTIONS

EFFORT

A conscious exertion of power.

Evaluate your effort based on the following scale

1 Strongly Disagree → 5 Strongly Agree

DAY:	1	2	3	4	5	6	7
I did all I could without holding back.							
I executed the most essential tasks.							
I raised my basis.							
I invested effort in my growth.							
I didn't spend major time on minor things.							
I said "no" to low-return things.							
I gave all-out efforts in my various life arenas: family, exercise, and so on.							

OBSERVATIONS & REFLECTIONS

DISCIPLINE

An activity, regimen, or exercise that builds a skill, habit, or attitude.

Evaluate your discipline based on the following scale

1 Strongly Disagree → 5 Strongly Agree

DAY:	1	2	3	4	5	6	7
I executed my pre-work mindset and/or exercise routine.							
I executed commitments regardless of how I felt.							
I said “no” to shortcuts and instant gratification.							
I spent less time with undisciplined “surfing.”							
I said “no” to excessive trivial pursuits: idle conversation, waiting/wishing/whining.							
I got off track less often than yesterday.							
I stayed off track for less time than yesterday.							

OBSERVATIONS & REFLECTIONS

INTELLIGENCE

The ability to acquire and apply skills and knowledge.

Evaluate your intelligence based on the following scale

1 Strongly Disagree → 5 Strongly Agree

DAY:	1	2	3	4	5	6	7
I acquired new knowledge.							
I practiced or improved a skill.							
I asked for feedback.							
I acted on feedback.							
I executed my action plan well.							
I tried something new.							
I learned from a mistake.							

OBSERVATIONS & REFLECTIONS

TENACITY

The quality of being very determined; resolved, relentlessly persistent.

Evaluate your tenacity based on the following scale

1 Strongly Disagree → 5 Strongly Agree

DAY:	1	2	3	4	5	6	7
I stayed on track despite obstacles.							
I persisted through tasks with excellence despite distractions.							
I kept going when I felt like quitting.							
I made myself do something when I didn't feel like it.							
I refused to take "no" for an answer today when pursuing a goal.							
I was unfazed by critics or rejection.							
I had encouraging self-talk.							

OBSERVATIONS & REFLECTIONS

ENERGY

Evaluate your energy based on the following scale

1 Strongly Disagree → 5 Strongly Agree

The strength and vitality necessary for sustained physical and MENTAL activity.

DAY:	1	2	3	4	5	6	7
I increased mental strength by building and guarding my mind throughout the day.							
I didn't engage in activities last night that drained my energy today.							
I had high levels of energy and engagement in all life arenas.							
I stayed mentally locked into the tasks that mattered most.							
I powered through when physically tired without "resting" at work.							
I avoided energy leaks.							
I ate energizing food and stayed hydrated.							

OBSERVATIONS & REFLECTIONS

____

____

____

____

____

____

DRIVE

An innate biologically determined urge to attain a goal or satisfy a need.

Evaluate your drive based on the following scale

1 Strongly Disagree → 5 Strongly Agree

DAY:	1	2	3	4	5	6	7
I did a quality job reviewing my *WHY*.							
I chose and reviewed my landing place.							
I didn't require external motivation.							
I focused enough on the goals that matter most.							
I focused enough on what I can control.							
I felt unstoppable today despite conditions.							
I avoided undriven people and drive-draining activities.							

OBSERVATIONS & REFLECTIONS

ACKNOWLEDGMENTS

So as to not turn this page into the written version of an Academy Awards acceptance filibuster ("I'd like to thank my agent, Slick; Cheryl, my sixth wife; my goldfish, Gilbert; and wiener dog, Wiggles"), I'll prioritize recognizing the unmatched contribution to this book's completion by my general manager and podcast producer, Ryan "The Killer" Cota. Thank you, my UNFAZED friend, for your unwavering loyalty and excellence in all things.

NOTES

1 "Intentional: Definition of Intentional by Oxford Dictionary on Lexico.com." *Lexico Dictionaries*. Accessed July 16, 2020, www.lexico.com/en/definition/intentional.
2 "Mindset: Definition of Mindset by Oxford Dictionary on Lexico.com." *Lexico Dictionaries*. Accessed July 16, 2020, www.lexico.com/en/definition/mindset.
3 "Killer Instinct: Definition of Killer Instinct by Merriam-Webster." *Merriam-Webster.com Dictionary*. Accessed July 16, 2020, www.merriam-webster.com/dictionary/killer%20 instinct.
4 Benjamin Franklin, *Benjamin Franklin's The Art of Virtue, His Formula for Successful Living*, ed. George L. Rogers (Eden Prairie, MN: Acorn Publishing, 1996), 10.
5 Franklin, *Art of Virtue*, 11; Benjamin Franklin, *The Autobiography of Benjamin Franklin* (New York: The MacMillan Company, 1901), 7, https://play.google.com/books /reader?id=qW4VAAAAYAAJ&hl=en&pg=GBS.PA7.
6 Franklin, *Art of Virtue*, 41–45.
7 Franklin, *Art of Virtue*, 45.
8 "George S. Patton Quote." *AZQuotes.com*. Accessed July 16, 2020, www.azquotes.com/ quote/531991.
9 Benjamin Franklin, *The Works of Benjamin Franklin, including the Private as well as the Official and Scientific Correspondence, together with the Unmutilated and Correct Version of the Autobiography*, compiled and edited by John Bigelow (New York: G.P. Putnam's Sons, 1904). The Federal Edition in 12 volumes. Vol. I (Autobiography, Letters and Misc. Writings 1725–1734). Accessed July 16, 2020, https://oll.libertyfund.org/titles/2452.
10 "Complacent: Definition of Complacent by Oxford Dictionary on Lexico.com." *Lexico Dictionaries*. Accessed July 17, 2020, www.lexico.com/en/definition/complacent.
11 "Drive: Definition of Drive by Oxford Dictionary on Lexico.com." *Lexico Dictionaries*. Accessed July 21, 2020, www.lexico.com/en/definition/drive; "Killer Instinct: Definition of Killer Instinct by Merriam-Webster." *Merriam-Webster.com Dictionary*. Accessed July 16, 2020, www.merriam-webster.com/dictionary/killer%20instinct.
12 Jim Rohn, *The Weekend Seminar* (Plano, TX: Jim Rohn International, 1999), DVD.
13 Ibid.

14 "Attitude: Definition of Attitude by Oxford Dictionary on Lexico.com." *Lexico Dictionaries*. Accessed July 30, 2020, www.lexico.com/en/definition/attitude.
15 "Tenacity: Definition of Tenacity by Oxford Dictionary on Lexico.com." *Lexico Dictionaries*. Accessed July 30, 2020, www.lexico.com/en/definition/tenacity.
16 *Respectfully Quoted: A Dictionary of Quotations Requested from the Congressional Research Service*. Washington, DC: Library of Congress, 1989; Bartleby.com, 2003. Accessed July 30, 2020, www.bartleby.com/73/.
17 Micah Potter, Twitter post, November 21, 2019, 2:24 PM, https://twitter.com/BigJam_23/status/1197641972665729024.
18 "Attitude: Definition of Attitude by Oxford Dictionary on Lexico.com." *Lexico Dictionaries*. Accessed August 3, 2020, www.lexico.com/en/definition/attitude.
19 "W. Clement Stone Quotes." BrainyMedia Inc. Accessed August 3, 2020, www.brainyquote.com/quotes/w_clement_stone_193770.
20 "Focus: Definition of Focus by Oxford Dictionary on Lexico.com." *Lexico Dictionaries*. Accessed August 3, 2020, www.lexico.com/en/definition/focus.
21 "Ralph Waldo Emerson Quotes." BrainyMedia Inc. Accessed August 3, 2020, www.brainyquote.com/quotes/ralph_waldo_emerson_101236.
22 "Compete: Definition of Compete by Oxford Dictionary on Lexico.com." *Lexico Dictionaries*. Accessed August 5, 2020, www.lexico.com/en/definition/compete.
23 "Leo Burnett Quotes." BrainyMedia Inc. Accessed August 24, 2020, www.brainyquote.com/quotes/leo_burnett_103239.
24 "Theodore Roosevelt Quotes." BrainyMedia Inc. Accessed August 10, 2020, www.brainyquote.com/quotes/theodore_roosevelt_120663.
25 "Quote by Sigmund Freud." Goodreads. Accessed August 10, 2020, https://www.goodreads.com/quotes/422467.
26 John Maxwell, *Developing the Leader Within You* (Nashville, TN: Thomas Nelson Inc., 1999), 153.
27 "Rigor: Definition of Rigor by Oxford Dictionary on Lexico.com." *Lexico Dictionaries*. Accessed August 10, 2020, www.lexico.com/en/definition/rigor.
28 "Lewis Howes Quotes." BrainyMedia Inc. Accessed August 10, 2020, www.brainyquote.com/quotes/lewis_howes_829600.
29 "Peter Drucker Quotes." Goodreads. Accessed August 10, 2020, www.goodreads.com/author/quotes/15162571.
30 "Robert Louis Stevenson Quotes." BrainyMedia Inc. Accessed August 27, 2020, www.brainyquote.com/quotes/robert_louis_stevenson_101230.
31 "Socrates Quotes." BrainyMedia Inc. Accessed August 10, 2020, www.brainyquote.com/quotes/socrates_101168.
32 "Zig Ziglar Quotes." BrainyMedia Inc. Accessed August 10, 2020, www.brainyquote.com/quotes/zig_ziglar_724596.
33 "Pin on Daily Calm." Pinterest. Accessed August 13, 2020, www.pinterest.com/pin/698058629583850731/.
34 "Winston Churchill Quotes." BrainyMedia Inc. Accessed August 13, 2020, www.brainyquote.com/quotes/winston_churchill_131188.

35 "Embrace Failure Quote." VeeroesQuotes. Accessed August 13, 2020, https://veeroesquotes.com/embrace-failure-quote-jenny-fleiss/.
36 "100 Inspirational Quotes on Self-Discipline." The Strive. Accessed August 13, 2020, https://thestrive.co/self-discipline-quotes-to-achieve-success/.
37 "Intelligence: Definition of Intelligence by Oxford Dictionary on Lexico.com." *Lexico Dictionaries*. Accessed August 17, 2020, www.lexico.com/en/definition/intelligence.
38 "Stupid: Definition of Stupid by Oxford Dictionary on Lexico.com." *Lexico Dictionaries*. Accessed August 17, 2020, www.lexico.com/en/definition/stupid.
39 "Moron." *Merriam-Webster.com Dictionary*. Accessed August 17, 2020, www.merriam-webster.com/dictionary/moron.
40 "Bruce Lee Quotes." BrainyMedia Inc. Accessed August 17, 2020, www.brainyquote.com/quotes/bruce_lee_413509.
41 "Bill Gates Quotes." BrainyMedia Inc. Accessed August 17, 2020, www.brainyquote.com/quotes/bill_gates_626252.
42 "Intelligence." *Lexico Dictionaries*. www.lexico.com/en/definition/intelligence.
43 "T. S. Eliot Quotes." BrainyMedia Inc. Accessed August 17, 2020, www.brainyquote.com/quotes/t_s_eliot_161678.
44 "Thomas J. Watson Quotes." BrainyMedia Inc. Accessed August 17, 2020, www.brainyquote.com/quotes/thomas_j_watson_209877.
45 "Salvador Dali Quotes." BrainyMedia Inc. Accessed August 17, 2020, www.brainyquote.com/quotes/salvador_dali_120513.
46 "Tenacity: Definition of Tenacity by Oxford Dictionary on Lexico.com." *Lexico Dictionaries*. Accessed August 17, 2020, www.lexico.com/en/definition/tenacity.
47 "Henry David Thoreau Quotes." BrainyMedia Inc. Accessed August 17, 2020, www.brainyquote.com/quotes/henry_david_thoreau_163655.
48 "Les Brown Quotes." BrainyMedia Inc. Accessed August 17, 2020, www.brainyquote.com/quotes/les_brown_389885.
49 "Mark Twain Quotes." BrainyMedia Inc. Accessed August 19, 2020, www.brainyquote.com/quotes/mark_twain_103756.
50 "Quote by Coco Chanel." Goodreads. Accessed August 19, 2020, www.goodreads.com/quotes/365652.
51 "Louis Pasteur Quotes." BrainyMedia Inc. Accessed August 19, 2020, www.brainyquote.com/quotes/louis_pasteur_133737.
52 "Energy: Definition of Energy by Oxford Dictionary on Lexico.com." *Lexico Dictionaries*. Accessed August 20, 2020, www.lexico.com/en/definition/energy.
53 "Dehydration: Definition of Dehydration by Oxford Dictionary on Lexico.com." *Lexico Dictionaries*. Accessed August 20, 2020, www.lexico.com/en/definition/dehydration.
54 "6 Dehydration Facts That May Surprise You," Drip Drop Hydration, January 21, 2015. https://dripdrop.com/blogs/news/6-dehydration-facts-may-surprise.
55 Ibid.
56 Ibid.
57 Ibid.
58 Ibid.

59 Ibid.
60 "4 Tips to Help You Attract the Right Kinds of Friends." Goalcast. Accessed August 24, 2020, www.goalcast.com/2017/08/07/4-tips-to-help-you-attract-the-right-kinds-of-friends/.
61 "Quote by Leonardo da Vinci." Goodreads. Accessed August 24, 2020, www.goodreads.com/quotes/476570.
62 "Napoleon Hill Quotes." BrainyMedia Inc. Accessed August 25, 2020, www.brainyquote.com/quotes/napoleon_hill_121336.
63 Wisconsin Basketball, Twitter post, March 7, 2020, 12:03 PM, https://twitter.com/BadgerMBB/status/1236381985406410758.
64 Wisconsin Basketball, Twitter post, March 7, 2020, 11:25 AM, https://twitter.com/BadgerMBB/status/1236372506543624193.
65 "Viktor E. Frankl Quotes." Goodreads. Accessed August 25, 2020, www.goodreads.com/quotes/29837.
66 "Seneca Quotes." Goodreads. Accessed August 25, 2020, www.goodreads.com/quotes/207438.

ABOUT THE AUTHOR

Photo by Hannah Peacock

Dave "Mr. Accountability" Anderson is a leading international speaker and author on personal and corporate performance improvement. After an extensive career in the automotive retail business, Dave, along with his wife, Rhonda, began LearnToLead (www.LearnToLead.com), now in its third decade, with the goal of helping individuals and organizations reach their personal and corporate potential.

The author of fifteen books and host of the wildly popular podcast *The Game Changer Life*, Dave's no-nonsense messages impact readers and listeners in over 145 countries. Dave speaks a hundred-plus times per year to a wide array of businesses, athletic teams, and nonprofits. He is the creator of REDBELT4M, a virtual training platform for amateur and professional athletes, coaches, and athletic staffs.

His direct, often humorous, and somewhat politically incorrect approach has earned him the nickname "Mr. Accountability," and his in-the-trenches background of starting and running world-class businesses, coupled with his relatable nonacademic approach, creates unmatched connection that resonates with his audiences and moves them to action.

Dave and Rhonda are also co-founders of the Matthew 25:35 Foundation, which helps feed, clothe, and house under-resourced people worldwide. In his personal time Dave enjoys the martial arts and holds a second-degree black belt in karate. He has been married over three decades to Rhonda, and enjoys life as a grandpa immensely.